MW00573305

Interest
Rate Risk
Management

The Banker's Guide
to Using Futures, Options, Swaps
and other Derivative Instruments

Benton E. Gup ■ Robert Brooks

IRWIN
Professional Publishing®
Burr Ridge, Illinois
New York, New York

A Bankline Publication

ISBN 1-55738-370-7

Printed in the United States of America

BC

3   4   5   6   7   8   9   0

Dedicated to Jean, Lincoln, Andrew, and Jeremy.

Benton E. Gup

Dedicated to Ann.

Robert Brooks

Table of Contents

List of Figures

List of Tables

Preface

What could be more timely than a *user friendly* book about derivative securities and asset/liability management (ALM)? Derivatives securities include futures, options, caps, collars, swaps, and more. They are making headlines, and are a major concern to bankers and others! "Derivatives Draw Warnings from Regulators," read a headline in *The Wall Street Journal* (March 25, 1992, C1). "Swaps: The Next Debacle for Banking?" was a lead article on the front page of the *American Banker* (August 4, 1992). Because of concern about derivatives, Section 305 of the Federal Deposit Insurance Corporation Improvement Act of 1991 (FDICIA) required federal banking agencies to revise existing risk-based capital standards to take adequate account of interest rate risk. The agencies must publish the final rules by June 19, 1993. Finally, the Office of the Comptroller of the Currency requires national banks to have a written policy with respect to managing interest rate risk.

This book explains how to use derivative securities to reduce interest rate risk for banks and other types of financial institutions. It is required reading for anyone involved in the use of derivatives or ALM. This includes bank directors, officers, and employees. It also includes bank regulators, accountants, and attorneys.

Being *user friendly*, this book can be understood by those who want only a general understanding of ALM and derivatives, but who are not interested in math and equations. In addition, it can be read and used by those who work with derivatives and want to know how to price them. We tried to write in "English" and to avoid math and equations wherever possible. The appendices at the end of some chapters contain the technical details and the math. Thus, readers seeking general knowledge should read the chapters; those wanting to know how to price derivatives, or other technical information, should read the appendices, too. An extensive glossary is provided at the end of the book for quick reference.

The book contains 11 chapters. The first two examine the effects of interest rate risk, and interest rate changes on the value of financial assets. Chapter three examines traditional and state-of-the-art ALM techniques. Chapters 4 through 9 explain how to hedge interest rate risks using forwards, futures, swaps, and various types of options. Chapter 10 explores some regulatory and accounting considerations. Chapter 11 contains the interest rate risk management policies of three banks. These are presented to illustrate how some bankers deal with interest rate risk.

The authors are indebted to Ira Kawaller, Chicago Mercantile Exchange, and to Frank M. Tiernan, Federal Home Loan Bank of Topeka, Kansas, for their helpful comments and suggestions. Any errors or omissions are those of the authors.

Benton E. Gup
Robert Brooks

Tuscaloosa, Alabama

THE IMPACT OF INTEREST RATES ON INCOMES AND VALUES

In the late 1970s, managers of banks began to recognize the importance of managing assets and liabilities simultaneously. They wanted to mitigate the adverse consequences of changes in interest rates, provide liquidity, and enhance the market value of their institutions. This chapter gives a brief introduction to asset/liability management (ALM), and it examines the impact of changes in interest rates on the income and value of banks. We use the term "bank" as a matter of convenience to include all organizations that are faced with interest rate risk.

A Brief History (1933–1970s)[1]

The United States Congress enacted the Banking Act of 1933, which, among other provisions, authorized the Federal Reserve system to regulate interest rates paid on time deposits. Furthermore, the Act prohibited the payment of interest on demand deposits. This legislation was passed in response to the banking panics of the early 1930s and other banking problems. During the period between 1921 and 1933, 16,305 banks suspended operations. Thus, the rationale for the legislation was to eliminate interest rate competition among banks, which was supposed to increase bank profitability and reduce the risk to the banking system.

Following passage of the Banking Act of 1933, interest rate competition among banks was not an issue because market rates of interest declined throughout the 1930s and early 1940s. Following the outbreak of World War II in 1941, the primary objective of the Federal Reserve was to facilitate financing the war. Accordingly, the Federal Reserve "pegged" interest rates on long-term government securities at a rate not to exceed 2.5 percent, and Treasury bills at rates less than 3/8 of 1 percent. Interest rates remained at low levels throughout the 1940s and early 1950s. The outbreak of hostilities in Korea in 1950 and growing inflationary pressures contributed to the "accord" between the Federal Reserve and the Treasury in March 1951, which ended the pegging of rates and marked the return to a free market. Subsequently, market rates of interest moved higher. Prior to the accord, bankers who had ample low-cost funds focused on asset management—the employment of those funds.

In the post-accord period, economic growth, financing the Vietnam War, monetary policy, and inflation spurred yields on U.S. Treasury bills. Returns ranged from 1.49 percent in 1951 to 14.71 percent in 1981. The increased rates of interest contributed to disintermediation, as investors withdrew funds from banks and invested directly in marketable securities beginning in the mid-1960s. The unexpected high rates of interest in the late 1970s and early 1980s was a major factor in the failure of depository institutions that borrowed high-cost, short-term deposits, and lent long-term at low, fixed rates. Large money-center banks, however, effectively hedged themselves against adverse movements in interest rates by matching the maturities, on average, of their asset and liability portfolios.

Financial innovations, such as negotiable orders of withdrawal (NOW accounts), Merrill Lynch's Cash Management Account, and money market funds, also caught the bankers' attention. In response to increased competition, bankers began to shift their focus from asset management to liability management. Bankers turned increasingly to certificates of deposit (CDs), and to nondeposit sources of funds, such as subordinated debentures, federal funds, Repos, commercial paper, and Eurodollars, for liquidity and to fund their growth.

Bankers also learned that interest rate ceilings, which kept their costs of funds low in earlier years, now restricted their ability to acquire funds. This problem was addressed by The Monetary Control Act of 1980, which included provisions to phase out interest rate ceilings on deposits.

Asset/Liability Management Defined

The term asset/liability management (ALM) entered the lexicon of banking in the late 1970s when bankers began to recognize the importance of managing both assets and liabilities simultaneously for the purposes of mitigating interest rate risk, providing liquidity, and enhancing the market value of their banks.[2] ALM is usually considered short-term in nature, focusing on near-term financial goals. Nevertheless, it is an integral part of a bank's overall planning process. This book deals with the impact of interest rate risk on incomes and market value of the banks rather than other corporate objectives. Examples of other objectives include responsible corporate citizenship, superior customer service, employee satisfaction, and so on.

Interest Rate Risk Defined

The last thing a referee says to boxers before they begin their bout is, "Gentlemen, defend yourselves at all times!" That is the basic theme of this book. Try your best to win, but defend yourselves at all times. "Defend against what?" you may ask. The answer is, "defend against interest rate risk." The Canada Deposit Insurance Corporation defines interest rate risk as follows:[3]

> Interest rate risk is the potential impact on a member's earnings and net asset values of changes in interest rates. Interest rate risk arises when an institution's principal and interest cash flows (including final maturities), both on- and off-balance sheet, have mismatched pricing dates. The amount of risk is a function of the magnitude and direction of interest rate changes and the size and maturity of the mismatch positions.

This definition provides a starting point for examining the effects of interest rate risk on your institution. In subsequent chapters, we examine various techniques for defending against the *adverse consequences* of interest rate risk. However, all interest rate risk is not bad. In fact, you can take advantage of desirable interest rate changes to increase the income and value of your bank. Before we explore that topic, let's examine interest rate movements in the United States and elsewhere.

Figure 1.1a depicts three-month Treasury bill yields from 1950 until 1991. During that period, three-month Treasury bill yields ranged from a low of about 1 percent to a high of 17 percent. The highest rates were reached in the early 1980s. Thereafter, yield declined.

Figure 1.1b shows monthly changes in the yields expressed in annual rates. A careful examination of the patterns reveals that changes in yields appear to be random. That is, they follow no predictable pattern. Past changes in yields cannot be used to predict future changes. The changes range from negligible to more than 500 basis points (5%). Large, unpredictable changes in interest rates do occur! That is why you have to defend against adverse changes in interest rates.

Large swings in interest rates are not unique to the United States. Figure 1.2 illustrates short-term interest rates in Japan, Germany, Canada, the United Kingdom, and the United States. Interest rate movements

Figure 1.1a   **Three-Month Treasury Bill Yields (1950–1991)**

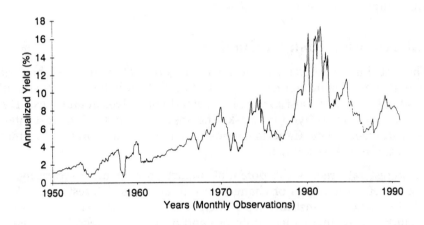

differ substantially from country to country. In recent years, interest rates declined in the United States. In contrast, interest rates in Japan and Germany increased sharply. In the United Kingdom they moved in a narrow range. In Canada, rates advanced, and then declined sharply. These diverse patterns of interest rates suggest that institutions borrowing or lending overseas face additional interest rate risks. Moreover,

Figure 1.1b   **Change in Three-Month Treasury Bill Yields**

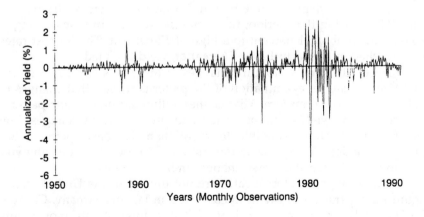

they face *foreign exchange risk*—the risk that there will be adverse changes in foreign exchange rates.

Investment Risk

Let's return to the definition of interest rate risk. The Bank for International Settlements (BIS)/Committee on Banking Regulations and Supervisory Practices states that interest rate risk has two elements: *investment risk* and *income risk*.[4] Investment risk arises when changes in interest rates cause changes in the market value of fixed-rate and off-balance sheet items. Investment risk is sometimes called *price risk*. As will be explained in detail in Chapter 2, there is an inverse relationship between changes in interest rates and the price of fixed-rate assets. In other words, when interest rates go up, the market value (price) of the fixed-rate assets goes down.

The BIS argues that investment risk should be considered an opportunity cost rather than exposure to actual losses except in the case of a forced sale. In theory, when the level of interest rates increases, low-yielding bonds are sold at a loss. The proceeds are then invested at current rates. The present value of the stream of income derived from investing at current rates will offset the loss. Therefore, in perfect markets, the impact on a bank's net worth should be neutral in the long term. However, accounting practices in most countries do not recognize this long-term neutrality; and trading portfolios are marked to market, which affects the bank's published net worth. The published net worth is different from the stock market valuation of the bank. Stock market values include attributes beyond balance sheet (and off-balance sheet) items. Such attributes include cash dividend payments, systematic risk (beta), franchise value, industry factors, and others.[5]

Suppose that a bank has mostly fixed-rate assets. If interest rates increase, the market value of the bank's assets will decline. If those assets are marked to market values, it will have an adverse effect on the bank's liquidity and published net worth. Bank regulators, who are concerned with safety and soundness, may consider closing a bank when it is illiquid and when its published net worth shrinks to unacceptable levels.[6] Federal bank regulators evaluate banks' interest rate risk management practices and procedures to mitigate such problems. Bank regulatory policies are examined in Chapter 10, and examples of interest rate risk management policies of selected banks are presented in Chapter 11.

Figure 1.2　　Short-Term Interest Rates—International

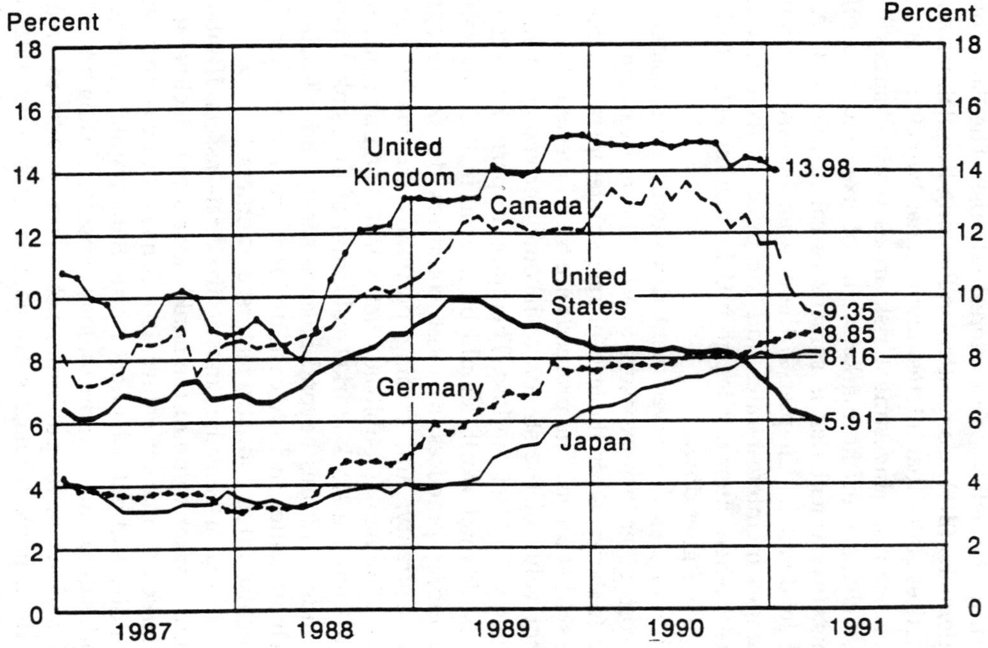

Prepared by Federal Reserve Bank of St. Louis

Income Risk

Income risk refers to the risk of losing income when movements in borrowing and lending rates are not perfectly synchronized. In banking jargon, it is a "gap" problem, which arises when there is a mismatch, in terms of time and interest rates, between repricing both assets and liabilities.

Assets and liabilities (both on and off the balance sheet) may be classified as rate sensitive, or non-rate sensitive, depending on their maturity and how often they are repriced. *Interest rate repricing* refers to the time when the interest rate on an instrument is adjusted. Some banks, such as BankAmerica Corporation, categorize certain assets by their expected repricing periods based on historical experience, rather than by their contractual repricing. The noncontractual repricing applies to certain consumer loans, deposits, and nonaccrual assets.[7] Assets and liabilities with one year or less to maturity are considered rate sensitive. Some assets with maturities up to five years or longer may also be rate sensitive.

The terms "fixed rate loans" and "variable rate loans" confuse the issue of rate sensitivity. The maturity and frequency of repricing assets determine rate sensitivity. For example, fixed rate overnight loans mature and are repriced daily; therefore, they are rate sensitive assets. By contrast, a variable rate 25-year mortgage loan that resets the interest rates once every three years is a non-rate sensitive asset.[8] Selected examples of both non-rate sensitive assets and liabilities, and rate sensitive assets and liabilities are shown in Table 1.1.

The Effects of Interest Rate Risk on Income and Value

Gap and Net Interest Income

In banking jargon, *gap* is the difference between rate sensitive assets (RSA) and rate sensitive liabilities (RSL) expressed in dollars.

$$\text{Gap} = \text{RSA} - \text{RSL} \qquad (1\text{-}1)$$

The dollar gap is widely used as a measure of interest rate sensitivity. When RSA exceeds RSL, a bank is said to be positively gapped. When RSA are less than RSL, a bank is negatively gapped. The dollar amount of the gap times the change in interest rates (Δr) gives the

Table 1.1   **Interest Rate Repricing**

Non-Rate Sensitive

Assets	Liabilities/Equity
Long-term fixed rate business loans	Time deposits (long-term)
Long-term securities	Fixed rate notes and debentures
Mortgages (fixed rate)	Equity capital

Rate Sensitive

Assets	Liabilities/Equity
Floating rate loans	Variable and short-term Federal funds purchased
Federal funds sold	
Short-term securities	Other short-term, variable rate nondeposit sources of funds

change in net interest income. *Net interest income* (NII) is interest income minus interest expense.

$$\Delta NII = Gap \times \Delta r \qquad (1\text{--}2)$$

For example, if a bank has a negative gap of $100 million, and interest rates increase by 50 basis points (+0.005), NII will decline by $500,000. Notice that the negative gap is preceded by a minus (–) sign. The symbol Δ means change.

$$\Delta NII = Gap \times \Delta r$$
$$-\$500,000 = -\$100,000,000 \times 0.005$$

If interest rates had declined by 20 basis points (–0.002), NII would have increased $200,000.

$$\Delta NII = Gap \times \Delta r$$
$$\$200,000 = \$100,000,000 \times -0.002$$

Interest Rate Spreads

Some financial managers think about managing assets and liabilities in terms of interest rate spreads. To illustrate the effects of interest rate risk on interest rate spreads, we will examine a small bank (with assets of $100 million or less) and a large bank (with assets of $1 billion or more). The proportions of their RSAs and RSLs are shown in Table 1.2. As a general matter, small banks tend to have relatively more non-rate sensitive assets and liabilities than large banks.

Using the following returns that can be earned on assets and costs of funds, the net interest spread is 3.8 percentage points for the small bank.

	Returns on Assets	*Costs of Funds*
Rate sensitive	12%	14%
Non-rate sensitive	17%	11%

The net interest spread was calculated by multiplying the interest rates presented above by the proportions of assets and liabilities shown for each bank. For example, the average return earned on the assets of the small bank is 16 percent.

RSA	$0.20 \times 0.12 =$	0.024
Non-rate sensitive	$0.80 \times 0.17 =$	0.136
		0.160 or 16%

Similarly, the average cost of funds for the small bank is 12.2 percent.

RSL	$0.40 \times 0.14 =$	0.056
Non-rate sensitive	$0.60 \times 0.11 =$	0.066
		0.122 or 12.2%

The net interest spread is $16.0\% - 12.2\% = 3.8\%$.

If short-term interest rates increase 200 basis points (2%), the net interest spread on the small bank will decline to 3.4 percentage points— resulting in a loss of 40 basis points.

We can get the same result by using a modified version of equation 2. Equation 3 indicates that the change in the net interest spread is equal to the gap (expressed in percentage terms) times the change in interest rates.

$$\text{Net interest spread} = \text{Gap}\% \times \Delta r \qquad (1\text{--}3)$$
$$-.004 = -0.20 \times .02$$

The small bank was negatively gapped as rates increased. Therefore, the smaller spread occurred because the proportion of the small bank's liabilities subject to the new higher costs is greater than the proportion of its assets on which the higher rates can be charged.

The net interest spread for the large bank is 1.5 percent.

Table 1.2   **Rate Sensitivity and Bank Size**

	Assets		*Liabilities*
Small bank RSA	20%	RSL	40%
Non-RSA	80%	Non-RSA	60%
	100%		100%
Large bank RSA	60%	RSL	50%
Non-RSA	40%	Non-RSA	50%
	100%		100%

Average return
RSA   0.60 × 0.12 =   0.072
Non-rate sensitive   0.40 × 0.17 =   0.068
                                                    0.140 or 14.0%
Average cost
RSL   0.50 × 0.14 =   0.070
Non-rate sensitive   0.50 × 0.11 =   0.055
                                                    0.125 or 12.5%

Net interest spread   0.015 or   1.5%

Because the large bank is positively gapped—rate sensitive assets exceed rate sensitive liabilities—it will benefit from the increase in interest rates. The net interest spread will increase to 1.7 percentage points, a gain of 20 basis points. Using equation 3, we get the same result.

$$\Delta \text{Net interest spread} = \text{Gap\%} \times \Delta r$$
$$0.002 \qquad\qquad = 0.1 \quad\times\quad 0.02$$

Effects on Value

The previous examples demonstrate that a bank's interest rate gap can affect its net interest income and net interest spread. If we assume that the value of a bank is positively related to its net interest income, we can illustrate graphically the effects of interest rate changes on bank values. The top panel of Figure 1.3 shows the effects of interest rate changes on a bank that is positively gapped (RSA>RSA; the symbol > means "greater than," and < means "less than"). If interest rates increase, the returns on assets will increase more than the costs of the

Figure 1.3   **The Effects of Interest Rates on Bank Values**

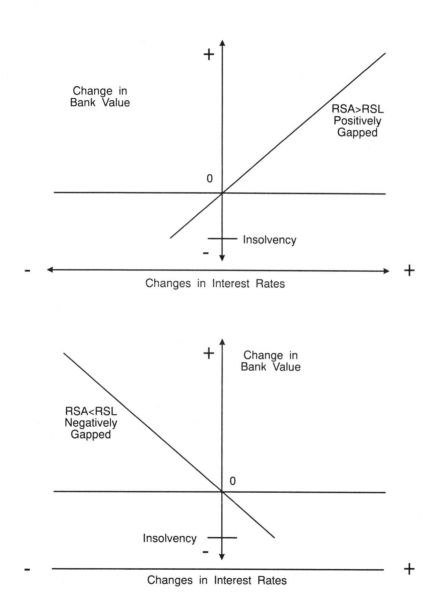

liabilities, thereby increasing the net interest income. As net interest income increases, the value of the bank increases.

If interest rates decline, the costs of the liabilities will exceed the returns on the rate sensitive assets, and the net interest income will diminish. The value of the bank can decline and it can become insolvent.

The lower panel of Figure 1.3 illustrates the effects of changes in interest rates on a negatively gapped bank. Rate sensitive assets are less than rate sensitive liabilities (RSA<RSL). If interest rates increase, the value of the negatively gapped bank will decline because its costs will exceed its returns, resulting in lower net interest incomes. However, if interest rates decline, the costs will decline more than the returns, thereby increasing the bank's net interest income and values.

Managing Interest Rate Spreads

Interest rate risk affects net interest income and the value of banks. For banks that are positively gapped, an increase in interest rates results in higher incomes and values. For banks that are negatively gapped, the reverse is true. This suggests that if banks gap correctly, they can increase their incomes and values.

Figure 1.4 shows one possible path of short-term interest rates over a business cycle. It also shows selected strategies to enhance income and values.[9] During the recovery phase of a business cycle, short-term interest rates are expected to increase as business concerns require funds to rebuild inventories and borrow for capital expansion. The rate of increase in interest rates tapers off during the prosperity phase of the business cycle. Interest rates peak, and then decline. During the recession, borrowers reduce their inventories, repay loans, and delay new capital expenditures. Rates decline further during the final phase of the business cycle, and then the process begins again. Although this is a simplified version of what actually happens to interest rates over the course of a business cycle, it provides a framework for examining spread management strategies.

During the recovery phase of the business cycle, banks should increase their rate sensitive assets, and attempt to lock in longer-term fixed cost sources of funds. Stated otherwise, they should be positively gapped. The positive gap should be the largest during this recovery phase of the cycle, diminishing in size as the business cycle matures. At the peak of the cycle, banks should lock in high-yield fixed rate loans, and obtain short-term variable rate sources of funds. It should be negatively gapped. The size of the gap should be the greatest during the recession and then diminish as the cycle approaches the trough. Then the process is started again.

This section demonstrated how banks may increase their net interest income and values by taking advantage of expected changes in the direction of interest rates. These strategies work if interest rates behave as expected and the loans are repaid on schedule. The key word is *if*. Recall that changes in interest rates appear to be random. Most of the monthly changes are small—less than 100 basis points when expressed at annual rates. However, in the early 1980s, some monthly changes ranged from 200 to 500 basis points.

In the late 1970s, few forecasters, if any, expected Treasury bill rates to soar from 5 percent to more than 17 percent. The high levels of the interest rates and the large changes contributed to the failure of

Figure 1.4   **Spread Management Strategies**

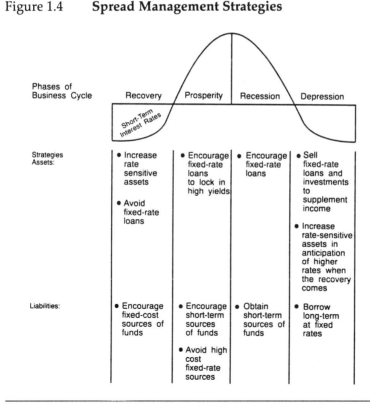

banks and thrifts that were not gapped correctly. Typically, these were institutions that invested long-term at fixed rates and borrowed short-term at variable rates. These failures suggest that large positive and negative gaps are risky. That is correct; they are risky. Managing a financial institution is the management of risk—interest rate risk, credit risk, liquidity risk, and other risks.

Three Methods for Dealing with Risk

In general terms, there are three methods for dealing with risk. *Avoiding risk* is the first method. For example, banks avoid credit risk by refusing to make certain loans that they believe are very high risk. They can avoid interest rate (price) risk by not investing in very long-term securities. *Reducing risk* is the second method. Banks reduce their credit risk by monitoring the behavior of their loans in order to detect the early warning signs of problems and defaults. Also, they reduce interest rate risk by using ALM policies designed for that purpose. *Transferring risk* is the third method, and the one that we focus on in this book. Buying insurance is one method of transferring risk from someone who does not want it to an insurance company that is willing to take it on for a price.

Today we have financial contracts and techniques available to transfer interest rate risk and allow institutions to have pro-active gap strategies. We call these financial contracts *derivative securities*. Derivative securities are derived (created) from previously existing securities. Put and call options, mortgage-backed securities, and swaps are examples of derivative securities. They derive their value from the value of the underlying stock, mortgage, or cash flow. We will examine derivative securities in great detail in later chapters. For the moment, it is only important to know that they exist and can be used to mitigate the unwanted part of interest rate risk.

Hedging is a technique used to transfer risk. The technical definition of hedging is "the initiation of a position in the futures market that is intended as a temporary substitute for the sale or purchase of the actual commodity."[10] We will examine the details of hedging in Chapter 5. For the moment, it is sufficient to say that hedging entails buying or selling derivative (and other) securities, in order to transfer risk. However, transferring risk is not free. There is a cost for trading derivative securities and hedging.

Let's consider the general effects of hedging on net interest income and the value of a bank. We begin by making the following simplifying assumptions: (1) All earning assets and liabilities are interest rate sensitive, and are repriced at the same time. (2) All bank earning assets and liabilities are fully hedged, or the bank is unhedged. (3) The effect of investment risk on the value of the firm is neutral. (4) In the long term, net interest income and the value of the bank are positively related to each other. In addition, we will only discuss a few of the many financial tools available for hedging. The practical reason for this limitation is the large number of combinations that can be generated. For example, there are 252 possible combinations for hedging ten assets, such as commercial loans, real estate loans, consumer loans, and so on, using five financial tools such as swaps, puts, calls, caps, and floors.[11] There are 2,118,759 possible combinations for hedging 50 assets using five financial tools! Another consideration is that the number of financial tools for managing short-term (overnight to six-months) interest rate risk exposure is greater than those available for managing long-term risks (five years or longer). For short-term risks, options and exchange traded financial futures may be the tool of choice. For long-term risks, long-term debt or swaps may be appropriate.

The top panel of Figure 1.5 shows changes in bank value on the vertical axis, and changes in interest rates on the horizontal axis. This is similar to Figure 1.3, which was explained previously. It shows that if a bank has a positive gap (RSA>RSL), the value of an unhedged bank will increase if interest rates increase, and decline if interest rates decline. If the latter occurs, the bank will become insolvent at some point. Some bankers believe that the optimal gap is zero, or slightly positive. We think otherwise. The optimal positive or negative size of the gap is dynamic, and it depends on the interest rate outlook and the degree of risk that a bank is willing to assume.

Banks can avoid the large losses by using symmetric or asymmetric hedges. A *symmetric hedge* is a gap hedged so that RSA is equal to RSL in order to minimize interest rate risk. This type of hedge provides a constant spread between returns on assets and interest costs, leaving NII unchanged. However, the value of the bank is increased because the risk is reduced. Specifically, a symmetric hedge is any strategy whereby both the positive and negative impacts of interest rate changes are reduced. This concept is illustrated graphically in the top panel of Figure 1.5. In this case, a swap is used to form a symmetric hedge. When interest rates change, the bank's value increases to the extent that risk is reduced. However, interest rate swaps may contain both interest rate

Figure 1.5   The Effects of Hedging Interest Rate Changes on Bank Values

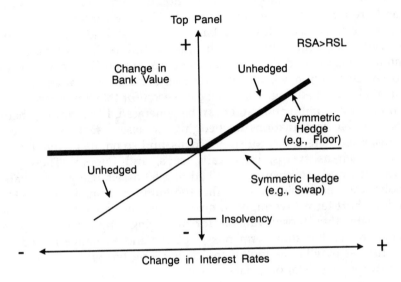

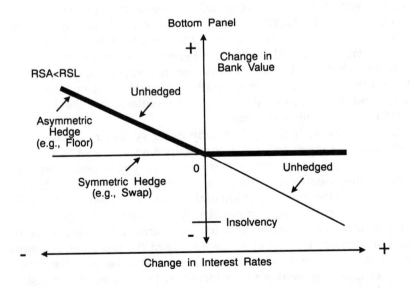

risk and counterparty risk; and they too may require hedging with futures, strips of Eurodollar futures, or by some other means.

Alternatively, banks can use an *asymmetric hedge*, where RSA and RSL are unequal. This type of hedge provides a variable spread between returns on assets and interest costs, resulting in increases or decreases in NII and the value of the bank. Specifically, an asymmetric hedge is any strategy whereby the positive impact of the changes in interest rates is preserved to some extent, while the negative impact of such changes is reduced. As shown in the top panel of Figure 1.5, the cost of a floor used to form an asymmetric hedge is represented by the shaded area between the unhedged position and the asymmetric hedge. This cost reduces the positive effects of increases in interest rates. However, if interest rates decline, the loss is limited to the cost of the cap. Thus, the advantage of an asymmetric hedge over the unhedged position is that the value of the bank would increase when interest rates increase, but would decrease only by the amount of the option premium if rates fall.

The lower panel of Figure 1.5 shows the value of a bank that is negatively gapped (RSA<RSL). In this case the value of the bank increases when interest rates decline. The costs and benefits of hedging are the same as in the previous examples.

Although not shown in the top panel, a bank could have a long net futures position to increase the interest rate sensitivity of its assets. However, there is a downside risk of being long in futures contracts because they can decline in value. Thus, except for the cost of the contract, the value would be similar to that of an unhedged bank. Expanding on this concept, the effects of net futures positions on interest rate sensitivity are shown below. A net long position means that the bank owns more futures contracts than it has sold. A net short position means the opposite.

	Net short position	*Net long position*
Asset	Decreases rate sensitivity	Increases rate sensitivity
Liability	Increases rate sensitivity	Decreases rate sensitivity

We can add a third dimension, time, to Figure 1.5. The time dimension is important because the degree of interest rate risk varies with the maturity of the exposure. Suppose, for example, that a bank has liquidity concerns in the short term, and wants to hedge its positive gap in the intermediate and long term. Using a time dimension, the bank may use a symmetric hedge to meet its liquidity needs for the first six months, and then use various asymmetric hedges to cover its longer-term gapped positions.

To Hedge or Not to Hedge? That Is the Question

Figure 1.6 is a schematic that may be used to evaluate the costs and benefits of hedging. The first step is to identify the risk. The next step is to determine if the risk is insignificant, significant, or intolerable. If the risk is insignificant, do nothing. If the risk is significant or intolerable, follow the lines, and answer the questions with a yes or no to determine which type of hedge to use.

Conclusion

Interest rates are a major determinant of bank incomes and values. Depending on a bank's asset/liability management policies and practices, a large change in interest rates can result in increased income and bank value, or it can result in disaster. The latter need not be the case. As we will see, derivative securities may be used to insulate the bank from adverse interest rate changes, and at the same time allow it to profit from desirable interest rate changes.

Figure 1.6   **Cost Benefit Schematic**

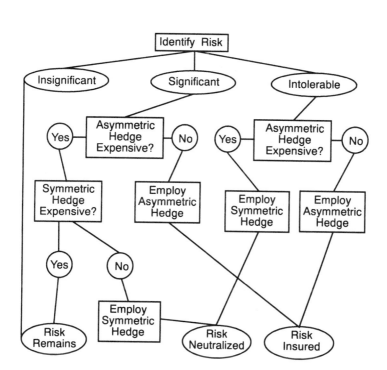

Endnotes

1. This section examines developments in the United States. For an international point of view, see R. Harrington, *Asset and Liability Management by Banks*, (Paris, France: Organization for Economic Co-Operation and Development, 1987).

2. Banks face other risks, including credit risk, foreign exchange risk, business risk, and others which are not covered here, but are important in terms of risk-based capital adequacy standards. For discussion of these risks and capital standards, see United States General Accounting Office, *International Banking: Implementation of Risk-Based Capital Adequacy Standards*, GAO/NSIAD-91-80, 1991.

3. *Standards of Sound Business and Financial Practices: Interest Rate Risk Management* (Canada Deposit Insurance Corporation, No Date, circa 1990).

4. Committee on Banking Regulations and Supervisory Practices, *Report on International Developments in Banking Supervision*, Report No. 6 Chapter VII (Basel, Switzerland: Bank for International Settlements, September 1988).

5. Some of these issues are discussed in connection with market value accounting.

6. The Comptroller of the Currency (OCC) also considers the market value of portfolio equity in assessing soundness. The *market value of portfolio equity* refers to the net market value, in the current interest rate environment, of an institution's existing assets, liabilities, and off-balance sheet instruments. For additional information, see *An Overview of Interest Rate Risk*, OCC Staff Paper, Comptroller of the Currency (Washington, D.C.: December 1989).

7. BankAmerica Corporation, *Third Quarter: An Analytical Review and Form 10Q* (1991) 36.

8. Although mortgage loans with such terms are not issued today, some were issued in the early 1980s and are still on the books of the lenders.

9. Based on work by Eugene A. Bonte and Gregg a Dieguez, "Spread Management: How to Maintain Profitability," *Savings and Loan News* (November 1979) 54-59.

10. *Commodity Trading Manual* (Chicago, IL: Chicago Board of Trade, 1985) 351.

11. The number of combinations C can be determined by: $C^n_x = n!/x!(n-x)!$, where n is the number of assets taken c at a time.

CHAPTER 2

UNDERSTANDING INTEREST RATES AND FINANCIAL ASSET PRICES

There would be no need for this book if we could predict accurately what interest rates will be tomorrow. Since we do not have perfect foresight, we will do the next best thing. This chapter (1) examines the major factors that determine interest rates, (2) explains the relationship between interest rates and financial asset prices, and (3) examines a theory used for forecasting rates. To examine the relationship between interest rates and financial assets, we focus on bond prices. Bonds represent credit instruments in general. They also represent financial assets of the investors who hold them. Most bonds are long-term credit instruments that contain a promise to pay both principal and interest on a loan on predetermined dates. Credit instruments include mortgage-backed securities, commercial loans, and so on.

Although there are technical differences between bonds, mortgage-backed securities, and commercial loans, the lessons learned from examining the behavior of bond prices may be applied to other credit instruments. For example, if a decline in interest rates causes bond prices to increase, the prices of other credit instruments will increase as well. The amount by which any of these increase in value depends on the interest rate paid on the underlying security, the general level of market yields, and the maturity of the underlying security. For convenience, we use the term *security* to include both investment securities and credit instruments. Finally, forecasting interest rates is both an art and a science. Part of the science centers on the "expectations" theory of interest rates. We will examine the expectations theory and its track record.

Interest Rates

The level of interest rates is determined by supply and demand for funds in the economy. Supply and demand, in turn, are influenced by monetary and fiscal policies as well as borrowers' and lenders' expectations about the future course of economic activity. With the exception of inflationary expectations, examining how these "macro" factors work is beyond the scope of this book. What we will do is examine the "micro" factors that affect bond prices. These include the term to maturity, time value of money (present value), and default and investment risk.

Interest Defined

Interest is the price paid for the use of credit. The terms *credit* and *money* are used interchangeably, but they have different meanings. *Money* is an asset of the one who possesses it, whereas *credit* is a liability of the one who possesses it. The following example will clarify this point. The amount of money (coin and currency) in your wallet is an asset because you own it. If you borrow funds to buy goods or services, the amount of credit extended is your liability. Interest is charged for the use of credit until the liability is repaid.

Real Interest Rates

Interest is the price paid for the use of credit, and the price contains two components—a real interest rate and an inflation premium. The *real interest rate* is the cost of borrowing without taking inflation into account. The *nominal interest rate* is the real rate of interest plus the inflation premium. The *inflation premium* represents the expected change in price levels as measured by some index such as the Consumer Price Index. For example, suppose investors want to earn a real rate of return of 10 percent, and the expected inflation rate is 8 percent. Lenders will charge a nominal rate of 18 percent to borrowers (10% real + 8% inflation = 18% nominal). The nominal interest rate will change if expectations about inflation change. If inflation is expected to decline to 4 percent, the nominal rate of interest will be 14 percent (10% + 4%).

Nominal interest rates can be misleading, particularly when income taxes and inflation are taken into account. For example, suppose that lenders are receiving a 15 percent return on their loan, they are in the 40 percent income tax bracket, and the inflation rate is 10 percent. As shown below, they have a 1 percent loss in real, after-tax terms.

$$
\begin{array}{rl}
15\% & \text{Return on loans} \\
-\ \underline{6\%} & \text{40\% income tax} \\
9\% & \text{Net to investors} \\
-\ \underline{10\%} & \text{Inflation} \\
-\ 1\% & \text{Loss}
\end{array}
$$

Investors who do not recognize the difference between nominal and real rates of interest operate under an *interest rate illusion*—the effects of inflation and taxes have reduced their real return.

Maturity

The relationship between interest rates (yields) and maturity (in years) is depicted in Figure 2.1. The connection between bond yields and bond prices will be explained shortly. This figure shows a Treasury *yield curve*, which is the relationship between yields on the y-axis (vertical line) and years when the securities mature on the x-axis (horizontal line), for fixed-income securities. Yield curves may also be constructed for corporate bonds, state and local government securities, and for mortgage-backed securities. Yield curves and yields on a variety of securities are published daily in *The Wall Street Journal*, *American Banker*, and elsewhere.

The yield curve shown in the figure is positively sloped. Positively sloped means that short-term interest rates (yields) are less than long-term interest rates. Notice the steepness of the curve for the first five years. Then rates increase at a slower rate for a few years, and finally they almost flatten out. This is the shape of a normal yield curve. However, yield curves take different shapes. At times short-term rates are higher than long-term rates. At other times intermediate-term rates are higher than both short- and long-term rates. Some investors interpret the shape of yield curves to help them forecast interest rates and bond prices. More will be said about that subject later in this chapter.

Present Value

Another reason for positively sloped yield curves is that lenders want more compensation when they give up the use of their funds for long periods than when they do so for short periods. The compensation for the use of funds over time gives rise to the notion of *time value of money* or *present value*. Present value is the current value of dollars that will be received in the future. In the context in which we are using present value, it is the current price of a bond. The following example will illustrate this concept. Suppose that you have the opportunity to invest in a hypothetical bond that will pay $10,000 when it matures in five years. It also pays an annual interest of 10 percent ($1,000/year). Most interest-bearing bonds pay interest twice per year. For simplicity, the bond used

Figure 2.1   Yields of Treasury Securities, June 28, 1991

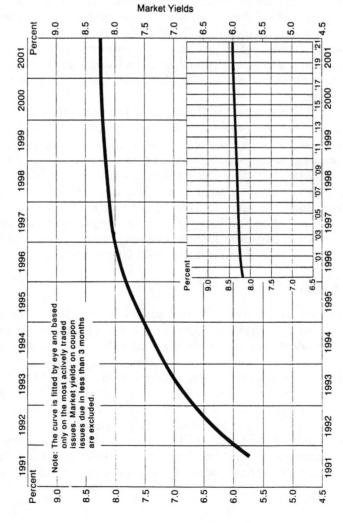

Market Yields

Note: The curve is fitted by eye and based only on the most actively traded issues. Market yields on coupon issues due in less than 3 months are excluded.

Source: *Treasury Bulletin*, September 1991, 66.

in this example pays interest only at the end of each year. How much would you be willing to pay for that bond today? What is it worth?

Before we can answer that question, we must determine the rate of return that can be earned on other bonds of a similar quality and maturity. This is the rate of return that investors will require in pricing the bond in question. The required rate of return is called the *discount rate* that is used to determine the present value (price) of the bond. Unfortunately, finance jargon is confusing at times, and this is one of those times. In the case of bonds, the terms *required rate of return, discount rate,* and *yield to maturity* all have the same meaning, and are interchangeable. *Yield to maturity* is the average return (including interest income and capital gains or losses) over the life of the bond. Suppose that 10 percent is the required rate of return—the discount rate—the yield to maturity that investors require.

As shown in Table 2.1, a 10 percent discount rate means that one dollar received at the end of one year has a present value of $0.90909. In other words, you would pay only $0.90909 today in order to receive a dollar one year from now. Similarly, one dollar received at the end of two years is worth $0.82645 today.

Notice that the present value of one dollar is worth less each year in the future. At the end of year five, the present value of one dollar discounted at 10 percent is $0.62092. Also notice that as the discount rate increases from 8 percent to 12 percent, the present value declines. Stated otherwise, increasing discount rates (interest rates) result in lower present values (prices). The method for computing present values is explained in Appendix 2A at the end of this chapter.

Figure 2.2 shows the cash flow diagram of the hypothetical bond. It also shows the present values of the cash flows discounted at 10 percent. The horizontal line represents years. The vertical arrows pointing upward represent cash inflows. The cash inflows are the $1,000 interest payments paid by the issuer at the end of each year, and the $10,000 principal amount paid at the end of the fifth year. The interest payments

Table 2.1   Present Value of $1 Received at the End of Period

Years	8%	10%	12%
1	0.92593	0.90909	0.89286
2	0.85734	0.82645	0.79719
3	0.79383	0.75131	0.71178
4	0.73503	0.68301	0.63552
5	0.68058	0.62092	0.56743

Figure 2.2   **Cash Flow Diagram and Present Value $10,000, 10%,
              Five-Year Bond Discounted at 10%**

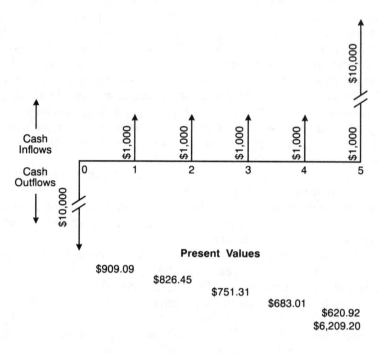

Present Values

$909.09

$826.45

$751.31

$683.01

$620.92
$6,209.20

$10,000 = $909.09 + $826.45 + $751.31 + $683.01 + $6,830.12

made by the issuer of the bond are cash inflows to the bondholder. The
vertical arrow pointing down represents a cash outflow. The $10,000 is
the present value of the bond. It is the price investors would pay for the
bond today.

The lower part of Figure 2.2 shows how the $10,000 price was de-
rived. The present value of the first $1,000 interest payment to be re-
ceived at the end of year one is $909.09. This can be computed by using
the figures presented above ($1,000 × 0.90909). Similarly, the $1,000 received at the end of two years is worth less ($826.45), and so on. At the
end of year five, the present value of the $1,000 interest and $10,000

principal is $6,830.12. The sum of all the present values equals $10,000, which is the price of the bond.

What happens to the price of the bond if interest rates change? As previously noted, the prices of outstanding bonds are inversely related to interest rates. If interest rates were lower, say 8 percent, the price of the bond would be $10,798.50. If they were higher, say 12 percent, the price of the bond would be $9,279.10.

Risk is another reason for long-term rates being higher than short-term rates. This is so because it is riskier to extend credit for 30 years than it is to do so for 30 days. Risk includes default risk, investment risk, and other factors.

Default Risk

U.S. Treasury securities are risk-free. *Risk-free* means that they have no *default risk*—the interest and principal will be paid. The Treasury will pay interest and principal on its obligations even if it must print the money to do so.

Because Treasury securities are risk-free, the yields on them represent the minimum return that investors require for a given maturity. Stated otherwise, investors extending credit to riskier borrowers require higher returns than they can get on Treasury issues of the same maturity. Otherwise, why take on the additional risk? Risk premiums, or the difference between the yields of risky securities and Treasury securities, are shown in Table 2.2. The Treasury long-term composite average yield is 8.37 percent. The yield on Moody's Aaa-rated seasoned corporate bonds is 8.92 percent. A *quality rating* is the measure of a borrower's creditworthiness. Aaa is the highest quality rating assigned to investment grade bonds. Bonds with Aaa rating have the smallest degree of default risk; both the principal and interest are well protected. The risk premium, which is the difference between the yield on the corporate bond and the yield on the Treasury security, is 55 basis points for the Aaa-rated security. The size of the risk premium increases as the quality ratings deteriorate. The A-rated bond, which is the lowest investment grade, has a risk premium of 112 basis points. The Baa, medium grade bond, has a risk premium of 169 basis points. The amount of the risk premiums varies over time.

For those interested in the technical aspects of pricing Treasury securities, Treasury bills are quoted on a discount basis. For further details see Appendix 2B at the end of the chapter.

Table 2.2   **Bond Yields and the Risk Premium**

Treasury long-term composite[1]	*8.37%*	*Risk Premium over Treasury*
Moody's Corporate bonds Seasoned issues		
Aaa	8.92%	0.55
Aa	9.23	0.86
A	9.49	1.12
Baa	10.06	1.69

Investment Risk

Although U.S. Treasury securities are default risk-free, they do have investment risk. *Investment risk* was defined in the previous chapter as a change in market values of fixed-rate and off-balance sheet items due to a change in interest rates. The terms *investment risk* and *market (or price) risk* are interchangeable. The amount of market risk depends on the maturity of the underlying security and the interest rate paid on it. By way of illustration, consider a bond which pays 10 percent interest per year until it matures. The bond has a $1,000 face value (principal amount) paid at maturity. As shown in Figure 2.3, interest rates and bond prices are presented on the y-axis. Years to maturity are on the x-axis. If the current market rate of interest is 10 percent (which is the required rate of return), the price of the bond is $1,000, regardless of the maturity. The price is $1,000 because those who buy this bond are receiving the current rate of interest, 10 percent.

What happens if market rates of interest decrease instantaneously from 10 percent to 8 percent, a 200 basis point change? Now investors require an 8 percent yield to maturity. Because the interest paid on the bond is fixed at 10 percent, the price of the bond must change to provide the investors with their required rate of return. In this case, investors bid the price of the bond up so that the yield to maturity is 8 percent.

The amount of the price increase depends on the maturity of the bond. The largest price changes occur in longer-term bonds. When interest rates decreased, the price of bonds with 20 years to maturity increased $198 ($1,198). An investor buying the outstanding 20-year bond will lose $198 in value if it is held to maturity. This loss happens because the

Figure 2.3   **Relationship between the Market Price of a 10 Percent Bond with Various Maturities and Market Interest Rates of 12 Percent and 8 Percent[a]**

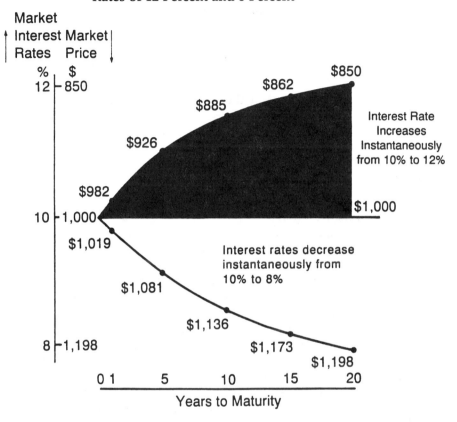

[a] Based on semiannual interest payments.

principal amount paid at maturity is $1,000. However, the combination of the $100 interest per year, less the $150 loss, averaged over the life of the bond, provides an 8 percent yield to maturity.

The figure shows that the price of bonds with five years to maturity increases $81, and bonds with one year to maturity increase $19.

If market rates of interest increase from 10 percent to 12 percent, the price of bonds will decrease. The price of bonds with 20 years to maturity decreases $150 ($850). The prices of bonds with five years and one year to maturity decrease $74 and $18, respectively.

These examples illustrate three important lessons:

1. There is an inverse relationship between market rates of interest and the price of outstanding bonds. Investors bid the prices of bonds up or down in order to get their required yield to maturity.

2. When interest rates change, the prices of longer-term obligations are more volatile than those with shorter terms to maturity.

3. The dollar amount of the price changes in response to a 200 basis point change in interest rates is not symmetrical. Price increases were larger than price decreases.

There are two additional points concerning bond prices that you should know:[2]

1. Bonds with low coupons have greater volatility than those with high coupons.

2. The higher the level of yields from which yield changes start, the greater the volatility of the bonds.

The previous examples of investment risk may give the *wrong* impression that the difference between short-term and intermediate- or long-term rates of the same class of securities (i.e., Treasury securities) is constant when market rates of interest change. The fact is that the differences (*spreads*) between rates on such securities change frequently. Figure 2.4 shows the yields on three-month Treasury bills, five-year Treasury securities, and other rates during the September 1990 to November 1991 period. The spread between the five-year Treasury security and the three-month Treasury bill was about 83 basis points in December 1990. The spread widened to 238 basis points in June, and then narrowed to 173 basis points at the end of the period shown.

Some participants in the futures market trade spreads. The futures market and trading spreads are examined in Chapter 6. Without going into details at this time, spreading activity includes the following spreads and others:

Figure 2.4   **Selected Interest Rates**

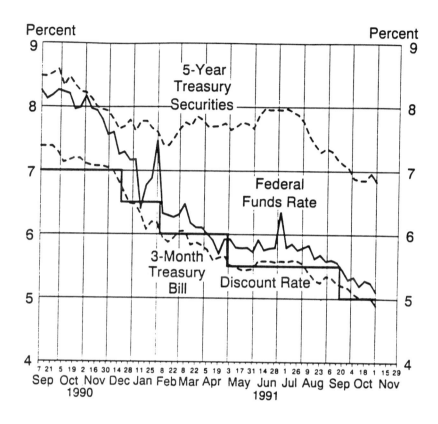

Prepared by Federal Reserve Bank of St. Louis

SPREADS	FUTURES CONTRACTS
TED	3-month Treasury bill futures versus 3-month Eurodollar time deposit
LED	1-month LIBOR futures contract versus 3-month Eurodollar time deposit
NOB	10-year Treasury note versus Treasury bond
FOB	5-year Treasury note versus Treasury bond

Stripping Bonds

The term *bond* was defined previously as a long-term credit instrument that contains a promise to pay both principal and interest on a loan on predetermined dates. However, some bonds pay no interest, and others never pay the principal amount. Therefore, it is difficult to capture the meaning of a bond in one definition because there are so many exceptions. Nevertheless, by examining the two polar extreme types of bonds—zero coupons and perpetuals—we will learn more about how bond prices are determined.

Zero Coupon Securities

A zero coupon bond is one that does not make periodic interest payments. The term *coupon* comes from the fact that on some bonds, interest is obtained by clipping coupons that are attached to the bond and redeeming them for payment. There are no coupons or interest payments on zero coupon bonds. The interest is built into their price. The bonds are sold at a discount and investors receive the face value of the obligation when it matures. The face value of most bonds is $1,000. The term *discount* means that the bond is selling below face value, and the term *premium* means that it is selling above face value. The required yield to maturity—interest rate—determines the amount of the discount.

Refer to Figure 2.5, which explains the concept of present value. From this figure we learned that the current price of the bond is the sum of the present values of the interest payments and the principal amounts. Investment bankers can *strip a bond* into its cash flow components—interest payments and principal amount—and they sell each component individually. The individual components are called *zero coupon bonds*. The price of a zero coupon bond is the present value of the cash flow. For example, the price of a $1,000 zero coupon bond maturing in one year, discounted at 10 percent, is $909.09. The price of a $1,000 zero coupon bond maturing in two years, discounted at 10 percent, is $826.45. The price of a $10,000 zero coupon bond maturing in five years, discounted at 10 percent, is $6,209.20—this was the principal amount of the bond being stripped.

Figure 2.5   **Cash Flow Diagram and Present Value $10,000, 10%, Five-Year Bond Discounted at 10%**

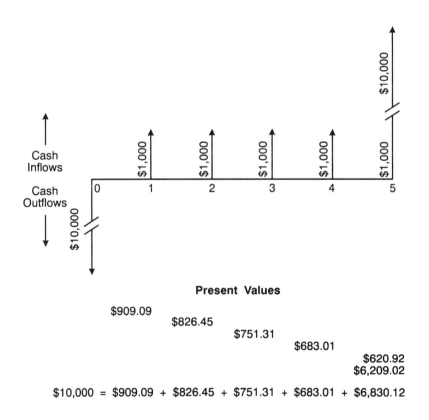

Present Values

$909.09

$826.45

$751.31

$683.01

$620.92
$6,209.02

$10,000 = $909.09 + $826.45 + $751.31 + $683.01 + $6,830.12

The U.S. Treasury sells stripped bonds too. Treasury coupon strips are called STRIPS, which is an acronym for Separate Trading of Registered Interest and Principal Securities. The Treasury STRIPS have a maturity of at least ten years. Some brokers market zero coupon securities representing interest and principal payments on U.S. Treasury securities. The brokers use proprietary names such as TIGRs (Treasury Investment Growth Receipts, Merrill Lynch), CATs (Certificate of Accrual on Treasury Securities, Salomon Brothers), and others.

As previously mentioned, what we learn about bonds can be applied to other assets. Let's consider *collateralized mortgage obligations (CMOs)*. These are derivative securities created from mortgage-backed bonds, primarily issued by the Federal National Mortgage Association and the Federal Home Loan Mortgage Association. Investment bankers strip the bonds into cash flow *tranches*, which refers to the various interest and principal payments. CMOs include various combinations of tranches. The structure of different CMO issues varies widely. In addition, there are *interest only (IOs)*, and *principal only (POs)* payments, which are zero coupon type securities. Those CMOs with more distant promises of payments in the future are risker than those with near-term payments. The reason is that, unlike typical bonds, CMOs may be prepaid when homeowners pay off their mortgage loans. *Prepayment risk*, or *call risk*, depends on a variety of factors, including the level of interest rates. When interest rates fall sharply, homeowners with high interest rate mortgage loans refinance them at lower rates. Thus, a mortgage loan with an original maturity of 25 years may be prepayed within one or two years. The average life of CMOs ranges from about seven to ten years, depending on the course of market rates of interest. The probability of prepayment depends on the maturity of the cash flow (tranche).[3] Longer-term tranches are more likely to be prepaid than short-term tranches. Therefore the structure of the CMO determines the likelihood of repayment. Accordingly, investment bankers can strip the bond, and then repackage various tranches to create new securities to meet investors' unique cash flow needs.

Perpetual Bonds and Preferred Stock

In the eighteenth century, the English government sold consols, or perpetual bonds that never mature, to help finance their war effort. The consols are still outstanding. In some respects, they are similar to preferred stock. *Preferred stock* is a form of ownership that has a preference of dividends or assets, if the firm is dissolved, over the common stock holders. Some preferred stocks are classified on balance sheets "quasi-debt," or *transient preferreds* because they have characteristics of both debt and equity. Transient preferreds are non-voting, have mandatory redemption, and are cumulative. Cumulative means that all dividends on the preferred stock that were not paid in the past, and current dividends on that stock, must be paid before the common stockholders receive any dividends. Some banks and other financial institutions issue preferred stocks as part of their capital structure.

The price (P_0) of preferred stocks is determined by dividing the dividend (D_0) by the investors' required rate of return (r). This pricing model does not apply to transient preferreds. Suppose the current dividend on the preferred stock is ten dollars and investors require a 15 percent rate of return. The price of the preferred is $66.67.

$$P_0 \quad = \quad D_0/r \qquad\qquad (2\text{--}1)$$
$$= \quad \$10/0.15 = \$66.67$$

If investors' required rate of return declines to 10 percent, the price of the preferred will increase to $100.

$$P_0 \quad = \quad \$10/0.10 = \$100$$

A Primer on Interpreting Yield Curves

The *expectations theory* of interest rates is the starting point for this primer on interpreting the shape of yield curves. The expectations theory is an economic theory which is an abstraction of reality—a simplified model. Economic theories help us understand how the "real world" works. However, since economic theories are abstractions, they do not provided precise results. But as we shall see shortly, they come close.

Without covering all of the details, the expectations theory postulates that long-term interest rates are an average of intervening short-term rates. In addition, investors are indifferent between holding long-term or short-term debt securities (bonds), as long as they obtain their required rate of return. The return that they expect to receive depends mostly on the price of the bonds.

Figure 2.6 shows two yield curves in the top panel. The normal yield curve is shaped like the one shown in Figure 2.1, which was discussed previously. The positive sloping yield curve is much steeper than the normal yield curve. According to the theory, the steeper positively shaped yield curve suggests that long-term interest rates are going to rise. Investors believing this to be so will sell long-term bonds to avoid price losses. When market rates of interest rise, the price losses are the greatest for long-term bonds. By selling the long-term bonds, they force the price down, and the interest rates up. These same investors use those funds to buy short-term debt securities. When they buy the short-term securities, they bid the price up, and the interest rates down. Hence the shape of the yield curve is positively sloped—low short-term rates and high long-term rates.

The lower panel of Figure 2.6 shows a negatively sloped yield curve. The theory suggests that long-term rates will tend to decline. Investors who expect long-term rates to decline will sell short-term securities, which depresses their prices and forces their yield up. They will use the funds to buy long-term securities that they believe will appreciate in value. Their purchases, in fact, force the prices of long-term securities up and their yields down.

To some extent, the shape of yield curves is related to business activity. Figure 2.7 shows a hypothetical business cycle and the behavior of long-term and short-term interest rates. During the recovery phase and prosperity phase of the business cycle, interest rates tend to rise because of the increased demands of business, households, and government to finance the purchases of goods and services. During the recovery phase, long-term rates are higher than short-term rates, giving rise to a positively sloped yield curve. However, as the business cycle evolves, short-term rates rise and exceed long-term rates, signaling that investors believe that a downturn in long-term rates may occur.

When business activity declines in the recession and depression phases, the demand for funds slackens, and interest rates decline. During the depression phase, short-term rates fall well below long-term rates, suggesting that a new cycle is about to begin. The changing relationship between long-term and short-term rates provides many opportunities for spread trading.

How well does this theory work? A study by the Federal Reserve Bank of San Francisco provides the answer.[4] Before each of the last four recessions (cycles peaked during 1969, 1973, 1980, 1981), the spread between the ten-year Treasury rate and the three-month Treasury rate turned negative. In the 1957 and 1960 recessions, the spreads narrowed, but remained slightly positive. Prior to those two recessions, the only time that a recession did not follow a negative yield curve was in the mid-1960s. Real economic activity did slow, but not to the point of being declared a recession. In February 1989, the yield curve was inverted for

Figure 2.6   **Yield Curves**

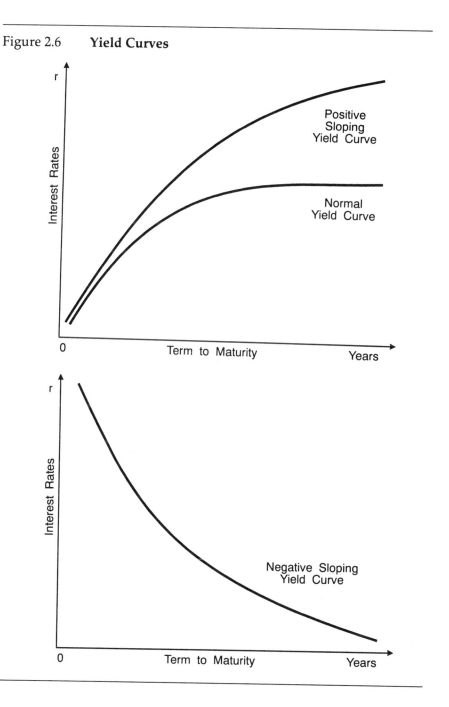

Figure 2.7   **Yield Curves and Business Cycles**

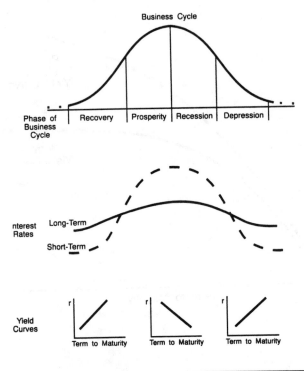

---

maturities beyond two years. This inversion signaled that a recession was forthcoming.

Conclusion

In this chapter, bonds were used to illustrate the effects of changes in interest rates on the price of financial assets in general. We distinguished between real and nominal rate of interest. The principal micro factors affecting nominal interest rates are maturity of the credit instruments, time value of money, and risk. Credit instruments have both default risk and investment (market price) risk. All of these factors are interrelated. Nevertheless, it is possible to "unbundle" some of the factors by stripping credit instruments, such as mortgage-backed bonds, and creating zero coupon type securities (eg., IOs, POs). Finally, the expectations theory of interest rates was presented to provided a framework for forecasting interest rates.

Endnotes

1. *Federal Reserve Bulletin* (June 1991) A23.

2. For additional information on these points, see Sydney Homer and Martin L. Leibowitz, *Inside the Yield Book* (Englewood Cliffs, N.J.: Prentice Hall, 1972) Chapter 3.

3. For details on prepayment experience and calculations on prepayment rates, see Sean Becketti and Charles S. Morris, *The Prepayment Experience of FNMA Mortgage-backed Securities* (New York: New York University Salomon Center, 1990) Monograph Series in Finance and Economics, 1990-3.

4. Frederick T. Furlong, "The Yield Curve and Recessions," *FRSB Weekly Letter*, Federal Reserve Bank of San Francisco, March 10, 1989.

Appendix 2A

Calculating Present Values and Bond Prices

This appendix explains how to compute present values and bond prices. The current market price of a bond is the present value of its cash flows discounted by investors' required rate of return. The cash flows consist of interest and principal. For your convenience, the symbols used in this appendix are listed below.

Symbols Used in This Appendix

C	Annual income from coupons expressed in dollars ($)
FV_n	Future value or dollar amount at the end of the nth period
r	Interest rate per period (%)
I	Dollar amount of interest earned per period ($)
m	Number of payments per period
n	Number of periods
P_0	Market price ($)
PMT	Payment per period
PV	Present value, or the principal amount
PV_a	Present value of an annuity
V	Value of an obligation at maturity

Present Value

The equation used to determine the present value is:

$$PV_0 = FV_n \left[\frac{1}{(1+r)^n} \right] \qquad (2A\text{--}1)$$

Let's use equation 2A-1 to determine the present value of a $100,000 deposit to be made at the end of the second year. We substitute $100,000 for the future value in the second year, and discount that amount by 12 percent for two years. Accordingly, the present value is:

$$PV_0 = FV_n \left[\frac{1}{(1+r)^n} \right]$$

$$= \$100,000 \left[\frac{1}{(1+0.12)^2} \right]$$

$$= \$100,000\,(0.79719)$$

$$= \$79,719$$

The 0.79719 is the *present value interest factor*. Multiplying the present value interest factor by $100,000 gives a present value of $79,719. In other words, if 12 percent is the required rate of return, $100,000 to be received two years from now is worth $79,719 today. This example dealt with one cash flow payment. Next we examine multiple cash flow payments to be received in the future.

Annuities

An *annuity* is defined as a series of periodic payments that are made in equal amounts for a specified period of time. Interest payments on bonds are one example of an annuity. Understanding how to compute the present value of annuities is a time-saving device when determining the value of bonds. The type of annuity used here is called an *ordinary annuity* because the interest payments are made at the end of each payment interval and the term to maturity is specified (that is, ten years).

Suppose that you wanted to know the present value of an annuity that will pay $1,000 per year for three years, and the discount rate is 15 percent. One way to determine the present value of the annuity is to use present value interest factors and multiply them by the payments for each year. For example,

Years	Payments	×	Present value interest factors	=	Amounts
1	$1,000		0.88957		$ 869.57
2	1,000		0.75614		756.14
3	1,000		0.65752		657.52
	Totals		2.28323		$2,283.23

The sum of the present value interest factors is 2.28323. One can obtain the same answer with less effort by multiplying the periodic payment (PMT) of $1,000 by the *present value of an annuity interest factor* of 2.2832 derived from the following equation:

$$PV_a = PMT \frac{1-(1+r)^{-n}}{r} \qquad (2A\text{--}2)$$

$$PV_a = PMT \frac{1-(1.15)^{-3}}{0.15}$$

$$= 2.2832$$

For example, the present value of the three-year annuity discounted at 15 percent is:

$$PV_a = \$1,000\,(2.2832)$$

$$= \$2,283.20$$

Bond Prices

The price of a bond is computed by determining the present value of an annuity for the interest payments and the present value of the principal amount when it is paid. The combined equation used to determine the price of bonds is:

$$P_0 = \begin{matrix}\text{Present value of} \\ \text{interest payments}\end{matrix} + \begin{matrix}\text{Present value} \\ \text{of face amount}\end{matrix}$$

$$= \sum_{t=1}^{n} \frac{C}{(1+r)^t} + \frac{V}{(1+r)^n} \qquad (2A\text{--}3)$$

where
C   = annual income expressed in dollars
V   = value of obligation at maturity
r   = interest rate per period required by investors

48 CHAPTER 2

Equation 2A-3 is used in the following manner to determine the price of a bond. Assume that a previously issued bond with a 12 percent coupon (it pays $120 interest per year, $120/$1,000 = 12%) matures in ten years, and the current market rate of interest, which is the rate required by investors, is 9 percent. The face value of the bond is $1,000. The market price of that bond is:

$$P_0 = \sum_{t=1}^{n} \frac{C}{(1+r)^t} + \frac{V}{(1+r)^n}$$

$$P_0 = \sum_{t=1}^{10} \frac{\$120}{(1+0.09)^{10}} + \frac{\$1,000}{(1+0.09)^{10}}$$

$$= \$120\,(6.4176) + \$1,000\,(0.4224)$$
$$= \$1,192$$

Equation 2A-3 assumes that interest is paid once per year. However, most bonds pay interest twice per year. Therefore, the slight modification to the equation shown below permits us to make any number of payments per period m. If payments are made twice per year, m is two. If payments are made monthly, m is twelve, and so on.

$$= \sum_{t=1}^{n} \frac{\frac{C}{m}}{(1+\frac{r}{m})^{tm}} + \frac{V}{(1+\frac{r}{m})^{nm}} \qquad (2A\text{--}4)$$

where

m = number of payments per period

For example, if interest payments are made twice each year, the price of the bond is:

$$P_0 = \sum_{t=1}^{n} \frac{\frac{C}{m}}{(1+\frac{r}{m})^{tm}} + \frac{V}{(1+\frac{r}{m})^{nm}}$$

$$= \sum_{t=1}^{20} \frac{\frac{\$120}{2}}{(1+\frac{0.09}{2})^{10*2}} + \frac{\$1,000}{(1+\frac{0.09}{2})^{10*2}}$$

$$= \$60\,(13.0263) + \$1,000\,(0.4146)$$
$$= \$1,196$$

Appendix 2B

Treasury Bill Prices and Yields

Treasury bills are short-term obligations of the United States government. Although they may be issued with an original maturity of one year, most are issued with maturities of three months or six months. They are used extensively by institutional and individual investors because of their high liquidity and because they are *risk-free*—there is no risk of default. Nevertheless, the prices (and yields) of outstanding Treasury bills do vary when market interest rates change. However, since they are short-term securities, the prices are not as large as those of long-term securities.

This appendix explains the "traditional" method of calculating selected Treasury bill prices and yields. Today such calculations are performed for investors on calculators or computers, and investors may not understand how the prices or yields are derived. This appendix provides that explanation.[1]

Discount Price

Treasury bills are sold to investors at a discount, and they receive the face value when the obligation matures. The computation of the discount is based on a 360-day year. Since most bonds are traded on a 365-day year, we will calculate the "bond equivalent yield" (or the 365-day yield) on Treasury bills shortly. The equations for calculating the discount price are:

$$F = \frac{r}{360 \text{ days}} \times D_m \qquad\qquad (2B\text{--}1)$$

$$P_0 = \$100 - F$$

where

F	= full discount
r	= discount basis or interest rate
D_m	= number of days to maturity (or number of days held [days to maturity when purchased less days to maturity when sold, D_h])
P_0	= dollar price

To illustrate the use of the equations, assume that a Treasury bill has a 90-day maturity and that the discount basis (interest rate) is 13 percent. The price of the Treasury bill is:

$$F = \frac{r}{360} \times D_m$$

$$P_0 = \$100 - F$$

$$F = \frac{13.00\%}{360} \times 90 \text{ days} = 3.25\% \; or \; \$3.25 \text{ per } \$100 \text{ value}$$
$$P_0 = \$100 - \$3.25 = \$96.75 \text{ per } \$100 \text{ value}$$

Treasury bills are sold in denominations of $10,000 or more. Therefore, the market price of such a bill is $9,675. When the bill matures, investors will be paid $10,000 face value.

Bond Equivalent Yield

The bond equivalent yield Y for Treasury bills less than one year can be determined by:

$$Y = \frac{F}{P_0} \times \frac{365}{D_m} \times 100 \qquad\qquad (2B\text{--}2)$$

In the case of leap year, use 366 days.
The bond equivalent yield of the treasury bill is:

$$Y = \frac{F}{P_0} \times \frac{365}{D_m} \times 100$$

$$= \frac{\dfrac{\$3}{25}}{\$96.75} \times \frac{365}{90} \times 100$$

$$= 13.62\%$$

Holding Periods Less Than Maturity

Suppose the Treasury bill is only held for 15 days, and it is sold at a 12.5 percent discount basis. The yield for the holding period Y_h is determined by

$$Y_h = \frac{S - P_0}{P_0} \times \frac{365}{D_h} \times 100 \qquad\qquad (2B\text{-}3)$$

where

S = the selling price, and is computed the same as P_0

$$F = \frac{r}{360} \times D_h \quad (D_h = 90 \text{ days} - 75 \text{ days} = 15 \text{ days})$$

$$= \frac{12.5\%}{360} \times 15$$

$$= 0.52\% \text{ or } \$0.52 \text{ per } \$100 \text{ value}$$

$$S = \$100 - F$$

$$= \$100 - \$0.52$$

$$= \$99.48$$

Now using the value of S in equation 2B-3, the annualized yield for the holding period is:

$$Y_h = \frac{S - P_0}{P_0} \times \frac{365}{D_h} \times 100$$

$$= \frac{\$99.48 - \$96.75}{\$96.75} \times \frac{365}{15} \times 100$$

$$= 66.75\%$$

This annualized yield is very high due to falling interest rates during the period.

In summary, Treasury bills are risk-free short-term investments that provide investors with short-term, risk-free returns. Because the yields on Treasury bills are computed on a 360-day basis, investors should convert them to bond equivalent yields when comparing them to other investments. The bond equivalent yield is always higher than the Treasury bill yield.

Endnotes

1. For additional details on the calculations, see *Handbook of Securities of the United States Government and Federal Agencies and Related Money Market Instruments*, 33rd. (New York: The First Boston Corporation, 1988).

CHAPTER 3

TRADITIONAL ALM TECHNIQUES: STRENGTHS AND WEAKNESSES

Three ALM techniques are examined in this chapter. The techniques are gap analysis, duration analysis, and simulation. Each technique is used to deal with interest rate risk. And each technique has its own strengths and weaknesses.

Gap Analysis

Gap analysis measures the differences between the amount of rate sensitive assets (RSA) and rate sensitive on- and off-balance sheet liabilities (RSL) that reprice in a particular time period. As noted in Chapter 1, a bank is positively gapped when rate sensitive assets exceed rate sensitive liabilities. The net interest income (NII) of banks that are positively gapped increases when interest rates increase, and decreases when they decline. This is so because the bank is "asset sensitive." That is, interest income from RSAs increases more than interest expenses from RSLs. A bank is negatively gapped when rate sensitive assets are less than rate sensitive liabilities. Such banks are "liability sensitive." NII of negatively gapped banks increases when interest rates decline. If the gap is zero (RSA = RSL), there is no interest rate sensitivity, and NII is unaffected by changes in interest rates. The extent to which banks have positive, negative, or zero gaps depends on their operating strategy, the interest rate outlook, and other factors.

Periodic Gap Analysis Reports

Banks use gap analysis reports to measure the interest rate sensitivity of RSA and RSL for different periods. For this reason, it is sometimes referred to as a *periodic gap*, in contrast to a duration gap, which is explained next. The periods are also called *maturity buckets*. Some banks use maturity buckets based on the maturity and repricing data for loans, leases, and deposits that are reported in the Call Report Forms submitted to bank regulators. These periods are 0-3 months, 3-12 months, 1-5 years, and over five years. However, any periods may be used. Chase Manhattan, for example, groups its assets, liabilities, and off-balance sheet items into three groups: known maturities, judgmental maturities, and market-driven maturities.[1] Known maturities are contractually defined for fixed rate loans, CDs, and so on. Judgmental maturities are based on past experience for credit cards, passbooks, demand deposits, and nonperforming loans. Market-driven maturities are on all option-type instruments, including mortgages that may be prepaid if interest rates fall. Other banks use different periods, depending on their operating strategy. Table 3.1 shows the interest rate sensitivity analysis of Barnett Banks, Inc., presented in their 1990 annual report. Barnett Banks uses 0-30 days, 31-90 days, 91-180 days, and 181-365 days. Non-rate sensitive assets and liabilities and over-one-year maturities are grouped together in the final period shown. The data reveal that the bank has a negative interest rate sensitivity gap under 180 days, and is positively gapped beyond that period.

The *cumulative gap*, which is the sum of the individual gaps up to one year, is negative. Moreover, the negative $3,268 million cumulative gap is equal to the positive gap for the over-one-year period. Barnett's strategy is to offset their negative cumulative gap under one year with a positive gap beyond that period and non-rate sensitive assets and liabilities.[2] Thus, Barnett was positioned to benefit from the decline in interest rates which occurred in 1991.

Effect of Gap on Net Interest Income

Bank managers may use the cumulative gap to estimate the impact of changes in interest rates on net interest income (NII). The change in NII is equal to the cumulative gap times the change in interest rates. This is similar to equation 1-2 used in Chapter 1, but the cumulative gap is used here. Barnett's cumulative gap for one year and under is negative $3,268 million, and we assume that maturities of more than one year are non-rate sensitive. If interest rates decline, say 200 basis points, NII could increase $65.36 million.

$$\Delta \text{NII} = \text{Cumulative Gap} \times \Delta r \tag{3-1}$$

$$\$65.36 = \$3,268 \qquad \times 0.0200$$

This equation may also be used to test the sensitivity of different size gaps, or to determine what size gaps are necessary to produce a

Table 3.1 Interest Rate Sensitivity Analysis

December 31, 1990—Dollars in Millions	0-30 Days	31-90 Days	91-180 Days	181-365 Days	Non-Rate Sensitive and Over One Year	Total
Variable-rate commercial and real estate loans	$6,104	$11	$40	$14	—	$6,169
Fixed-rate commercial and real estate loans including ARMs	856	811	1,112	2,314	$5,510	10,603
Consumer loans	1,165	326	470	878	4,639	7,478
Total loans	8,125	1,148	1,622	3,206	10,149	24,250
Securities	767	229	104	214	2,921	4,235
Federal funds sold and other earning assets	180					180
Total earning assets	9,072	1,377	1,726	3,420	13,070	28,665
Cash property and other assets					3,960	3,960
Less: Allowance for loan losses					(411)	(411)
Total assets	$9,072	$1,377	$1,726	$3,420	$16,619	$32,214
Demand deposits					$3,763	$3,763
NOW accounts					3,642	3,642
Money market accounts	$4,788					4,788

Table 3.1   **Interest Rate Sensitivity Analysis** (continued)

Savings deposits					1,907	1,907
Certificates of deposit under $100,000	2,781	$1,992	$2,528	$1,840	$1,582	10,723
Other time deposits	1,472	806	848	537	240	3,903
Total deposits	9,041	2,798	3,376	2,377	11,134	28,726
Federal funds purchased and other short-term borrowings	1,120					1,120
Long-term debt	151				344	495
Other liabilities					300	300
Shareholders' equity					1,573	1,573
Total liabilities and shareholders' equity	$10,312	$2,798	$3,376	$2,377	$13,351	$32,214
Interest rate sensitivity gap	$(1,240)	$(1,421)	$(1,650)	$1,043	$3,268	
Cumulative interest rate sensitivity gap	(1,240)	(2,661)	(4,311)	(3,268)	—	—
Cumulative gap as percentage of earning assets at December 31 1990	(4.3)%	(9.3)%	(15.0)%	(11.4)%	—	
Cummulative gap as percentage of earning assets at December 31 1989	(2.8)	(7.9)	(13.3)	(8.8)	—	

aIf NOW accounts and savings deposits had been included in the 0-30 days category, cumulative gap as a percentage of earning assets would have been a negative 23.7% for this category at December 31, 1990.

Source: Barnett Banks, Inc., Annual Report, 1990, 23.

target change in NII. This type of analysis is best done with simulations which are discussed later in this chapter.

Assumptions and Limitations of Gap Analysis

The use of gap analysis is based on the following assumptions, which may or may not be valid depending on how banks calculate their gaps. One assumption is that the gap depends on contractual repayment schedules. If interest rates decline, early repayments of loans by borrowers refinancing at lower rates will affect NII. In addition, certain assets and liabilities have option-like features which borrowers and lenders may exercise as interest rates change. These include drawdowns of lines of credit and deposit redemptions. Early refinancing and the exercise of options affect the bank's cash flow. The cash flow does not distinguish between principal and interest payments. Another assumption is that all of the loan payments will be made on schedule. Some borrowers may make early payments, while others will default on their loans. Finally, gap analysis is based on the assumption of a parallel shift in the yield curve. That is, both short-term and long-term interest rates change by the same amount. If changes in the yield curve are not parallel, there is a basis risk.

Gap analysis has some widely recognized limitations.[3] One limitation is that it does not incorporate future growth or changes in the mix of assets and liabilities. Another limitation is that gap analysis does not take the time value of money or initial net worth into account. In addition, the periods used in the analysis are arbitrary, and repricing is assumed to occur at the midpoint of the period. Choosing different periods yields different results. Finally, gap analysis does not provide a single reliable index of interest rate risk. With respect to the last two criticisms, the critical measure of interest rate risk is the cumulative gap rather than the individual periods; and interest rate risk is multi-dimensional, involving both income and investment risk.

Gap analysis is used widely, despite the limitations of the assumptions, and the criticisms. One reason for the popularity of gap analysis is that it was the first method developed to deal with interest rate risk. Equally important, under some circumstances, it works reasonably well. Third, the data are readily available from the Call Reports submitted to bank regulators. Fourth, it does not require the use of a computer to determine the gaps. Fifth, it costs less than buying asset/liability management and/or simulation software. Finally, it is easier to understand than the theory and structure of duration analysis and simulations.

Nevertheless, both duration analysis and simulations are widely used to report interest rate sensitivity gaps.

One critic of gap analysis states that the maturity gap is a better measure of a bank's liquidity than its interest rate risk.[4] In the event of massive withdrawals of deposits, the rate of withdrawal is limited by the maturity of the deposits being withdrawn. Similarly, maturity also limits the rate at which assets can be liquidated to meet the withdrawals. He goes on to argue that a better measure of interest rate risk is needed. Next we examine duration, which is a better measure of interest rate risk. While duration is a better measure of interest rate risk than periodic gaps, it too has limitations.

Duration

The concept of duration was originated in 1938 when Frederick R. Macaulay wanted an alternative to the term *to maturity* for measuring the average length of time that an option-free (noncallable) bond investment was outstanding.[5] Duration is an index number that measures the interest rate sensitivity of any series of cash flows. The cash flows may be from individual bonds, stocks, mortgages, loans, or from portfolios of securities and loans. Duration takes into account both the timing and magnitude of the cash flows. In recent years, duration has received considerable attention from both academics and practitioners as a means of reducing interest rate risk.[6] The following discussion demonstrates how duration may be determined and used. Then we will examine how the assumptions for duration analysis differ from those of gap analysis.

Duration Defined

Duration is defined as the weighted average time to maturity to receive all cash flows from a financial instrument, such as a bond or mortgage-backed security. By way of illustration, assume that a bond has a $1,000 face value, the coupon interest rate is 12 percent (it pays $60 interest twice per year), and the term to maturity is 20 years. If the current market rate of interest is 12 percent, the duration of the bond is 7.97 years, which is about 12 years less than the 20-year term to maturity. In other words, the price of this bond will behave like a zero coupon bond with 7.97 years to maturity. Thus, when considering price changes, the concept of duration is used instead of maturity. This will be illustrated shortly.

Duration may be determined from duration tables or computer programs. The equation used to calculate duration is shown in the Appendix at the end of this chapter. Table 3.2 illustrates bond durations for selected coupon rates and maturities. For example, the duration of a zero coupon bond with ten years to maturity is 20 years. The duration of a bond with an 8 percent coupon and ten years to maturity is only 7.07 years, and so on. Five important lessons about duration can be learned by studying Table 3.2 in detail.

Lesson 1: Duration is less than term to maturity.

Except for zero coupon bonds, duration is always less than the term to maturity. In the case of zero coupon bonds, duration is the same as the term to maturity. This is so because the entire cash flow consists of the payment of principal at maturity, which is weighted by the year in which it is paid. There are no interim cash flows to be considered in a zero coupon bond.

Lesson 2: For bonds of the same maturity, those with high coupon yields have shorter durations than those with low coupon yields.

A 12 percent bond with 20 years to maturity has a duration of 7.97 years, while a 4 percent bond with 20 years to maturity has a duration of 13.95 years. This occurs because the interest payments from bonds with high coupon payments (12%) account for a larger portion of the total cash flow than interest payments from bonds with low (4%) coupon payments. Interest payments account for 70 percent of the total cash flow of the 12 percent bond and 44 percent of the total cash flow of

Table 3.2	**Bond Duration for Selected Coupon Rates and Maturities**[a]					
Term to Maturity (Years)	*0%*	*4%*	*6%*	*8%*	*10%*	*12%*
1	1.00	0.99	0.99	0.98	0.98	0.97
5	5.00	4.99	4.39	4.22	4.05	3.90
10	10.00	8.34	7.56	7.07	6.54	6.08
20	20.00	13.95	11.90	10.29	9.01	7.97
40	40.00	20.27	15.55	12.44	10.29	8.75
50	50.00	21.98	16.27	12.74	10.42	8.81

[a]Compounded semiannually.
[b]Assumes coupon yield equals market yield.
Source: Compiled from data taken from *Duration Tables for Bond and Mortgage Portfolio Management*, Publication No. 561 (Boston: Financial Publishing Co., 1980).

the 4 percent bond. Because of the present value weights given these interest payments in the calculation of duration, the high coupon bonds have shorter durations than low coupon bonds.

	4% Bond		12% Bond	
Interest for 20 yrs.	$ 800	44%	$2,400	70%
Principal	1,000	56%	1,000	30%
	$1,800	100%	$3,400	100%

Lesson 3: Longer terms to maturity mean higher durations in most cases.

Bonds with longer terms to maturity have higher durations than bonds with shorter maturities. However, the relationship is not linear, because as the term to maturity increases, the present value of the distant cash flows declines. The decline is particularly pronounced for high coupon bonds for reasons that were explained previously.

Lesson 4: Duration is inversely related to market yields.

High market yields result in a lower duration of outstanding bonds because the cash flows are discounted by higher interest rates. Consider the duration of a 9 percent coupon bond with 12 years to maturity. When the market yield is 9 percent, the duration of the bond is 7.57 years. When the market yield is 4 percent, the duration increases to 8.40 years, and when it is 14 percent, duration is 6.89 years.

Market Yield	Duration (years)
4%	8.40
6%	8.08
8%	7.74
10%	7.40
12%	7.06
14%	6.89

Lesson 5: Duration decreases as the frequency of payments decreases.

The timing of the cash flow payments affects the present value of those cash flows. More frequent payments result in lower durations because more cash flow is received in the relatively near-term.

Measuring Interest Rate Sensitivity

Bank managers can change their interest rate risk and improve their investment performance by using a duration strategy instead of a term to maturity strategy. For example, suppose that the prices of long-term bonds are expected to increase (interest rates will decline). The current yield is 8 percent, and it is expected to decline to 7.20 percent. Bankers wanting to profit from this information will buy long-term bonds. The bankers do not intend to hold the bonds for long periods. They have a choice of a 12 percent coupon bond or a 6 percent coupon bond, each with 20 years to maturity. Bankers using a term to maturity strategy might favor the 12 percent bond because it pays twice as much interest as the 6 percent bond. On the other hand, they might choose the 6 percent bond because bonds with low coupon rates have greater price volatility than those with high coupon rates.

Bankers using the duration strategy would choose the 6 percent bond. The 6 percent bond (with a current yield of 8 percent) has a duration of 10.92 years, while the 12 percent bond has a duration of 9.57 years.[7] Thus, the lower coupon bond, having a longer duration, will have greater price volatility than the high coupon bond.

The percentage change in bond prices that will occur with a change in market yields can be approximated by the following equation:

$$\text{Percentage change in bond price} = \frac{-D}{(1+i)/n} \times \Delta i \qquad (3\text{-}2)$$

where

D = duration[8]
Δi = change in yield in percentage points
i = yield
n = number of payments per year

To illustrate the use of this equation, we will use a 6 percent coupon bond with a duration of 10.92 years and a 12 percent coupon bond with a duration of 9.57 years. Interest is paid semiannually. Recall that market yields were expected to decline from 8 percent to 7.20 percent, a change of −0.80 percentage points. The percentage changes in the prices of these bonds prices are:

$$6\% \text{ coupon bond} = \frac{-D}{(1+i)/n} \times \Delta i$$

$$= \frac{-10.92}{(1.04)} \times -0.80$$

$$= 8.48\%$$

$$12\% \text{ Coupon Bond} = \frac{-D}{(1+i)/n} \times \Delta i$$

$$= \frac{-9.57}{(1.04)} \times -0.80$$

$$= 7.96\%$$

The actual price changes, based on bond value tables, are 8.9 percent and 7.8 percent, respectively. Thus, duration is only a linear approximation that works best when the yield changes are less than 100 basis points (1 percentage point = 0.01 = 100 basis points). The reason it works best for small yield changes is because of convexity. The term *convexity* refers to the nonlinear relationship between changes in bond prices and yields.[9] For very small changes in yields, the percentage price change is about equal to the change in yields. However, for larger changes in yields, percentage price changes are not equal. The extent to which the percentage price changes are not equal gives rise to an error in pricing. Bonds with call features cause additional pricing errors due to convexity. One may compensate for convexity, which results in a better approximation of prices changes.

Immunization

The previous section demonstrated that duration can be used when trading securities. It can also be used to lock in a yield for a certain planning horizon or holding period. A *holding period* is the length of time that an investor plans to hold a bond. Lawrence Fisher and Roman Weil developed an investment strategy that protects investors from changes in interest rates by matching the duration of the bonds with the length of their holding period. They said their strategy "immunized" bond portfolios.[10] Similarly, one can immunize assets and liabilities.[11] *Immunization* means obtaining a realized yield that will not be less than the yield to maturity for that holding period at the time the investments were made.

The basic idea of immunization centers on the fact that changes in interest rates have two effects on outstanding bonds, and they work in opposite directions. If interest rates increase, bond prices decline and reinvestment rates for coupon interest increase. The *reinvestment rate* is the market rate of interest. Stated otherwise, the coupon interest can be "reinvested" at the market rate of interest. Conversely, if interest rates decline, bond prices increase and reinvestment rates for coupon interest decrease.

To illustrate immunization, assume that an investor wants to receive $10,000 ten years from now, and that the funds can be invested today in bond A or bond B.[12] As shown below, bonds A and B have different coupons, prices, and maturities. The current yield is assumed to be 8 percent. For simplicity, we ignore taxes.

	Bond A	Bond B
Coupon	8%	6 1/2%
Yield	8%	8%
Term to maturity	10 years	17 years
Price	$1,000	$861.92
Duration	7.07 years	10.00 years
Number of bonds purchased at the current price	4.564	5.295

In order to receive $10,000 in ten years, the investor must invest $4,564 at 8 percent (compounded semiannually because interest is paid twice per year) for ten years.[13] The $4,564 will buy 4.564 units of bond A ($4,564/$1,000 = 4.564) and 5.295 units of bond B ($4,564/$861.92 = 5.295).

The investor has the choice of using a term to maturity strategy (buying a bond with ten years to maturity) by investing in bond A, or a duration strategy (buying a bond with a ten-year duration) by investing in bond B. If market rates of interest remain unchanged for the next ten years, which is unlikely, both strategies will produce the desired results if all funds are reinvested at 8 percent and the bonds are sold at the end of ten years.

No Change in 8% Market Yield

Term strategy
Buy 4.564 units of bond A

$1,000 (Bond price in 10 years) × 4.564	=	$ 4,564
$40/6 mo. (Value of reinvested coupons)	=	5,436
Total	=	$10,000

Duration strategy
Buy 5.295 units of bond B

$920.87 (Bond price in 10 years) × 5.295	=	$ 4,876
$32.50/6 mo. (Value of reinvested coupons)	=	5,124
Total	=	$10,000

A more likely case is that interest rates will change. Suppose that market interest rates change from 8 percent to 7 percent immediately after the bonds are purchased, and remain at 7 percent for the entire period. In this case, the term strategy results in a loss of $274, whereas the duration strategy results in a small profit. The increase in the price of bond B (the duration strategy) offsets the lower earnings resulting from the interest payments being reinvested at a lower rate (7%).

Market Yield Goes From 8% to 7% and Remains

Term strategy
$1,000 (Bond price in 10 years) × 4.564 units	=	$ 4,564
Value of reinvested coupons @ 7%	=	5,162
Total	=	$ 9,726
Loss	=	-$ 274

Duration strategy
$972.62 (Bond price in 10 years) × 5.295 units	=	$ 5,150
Value of reinvested coupons @ 7%	=	4,867
Total	=	$10,017
Profit	=	$ 17

Now let's see what happens when market rates of interest increase. Suppose that the market rate of interest increased from 8 percent to 9 percent immediately after the bond was purchased, and remained at 9 percent for the next ten years. The result is that the term strategy produced a $291 profit, whereas the duration strategy produced a $17 profit. A careful examination of the bond prices at the end of ten years and the value of the reinvested coupons explains the performance of each strategy. The duration strategy comes closer to achieving the desired results than the term strategy.

Market Yield Goes from 8% to 9% and Remains,

Term strategy,
$1,000 (Bond price in 10 years) × 4.564 units	=	$ 4,564
Value of reinvested coupons	=	5,727
Total	=	$10,291
Profit	=	$ 291

Duration strategy,
872.14 (Bond price in 10 years) × 5.295 units	=	$ 4,618
Value of reinvested coupons	=	5,399
Total	=	$10,017
Profit	=	$ 17

Rebalancing

The previous examples were simplified because only one change in market rates of interest occurred during the investment period, and the term structure of interest rates (yield curve) was flat. In reality, changes occur daily, and the term structure of interest rates is rarely flat. Therefore, investments have to be *rebalanced*. Rebalancing is also necessary to deal with the problem of duration drift. *Duration drift* occurs with the passage of time, and a bond's duration gets shorter as it approaches maturity.

The more frequent the rebalancing, the more likely one is to achieve the target returns. Semiannual rebalancing produces superior results to annual rebalancing. However, rebalancing too frequently may create more problems than it solves. One authority suggests that rebalancing should not only be based on the passage of time, but should also be triggered by certain interest rate movements, and by events such as changes in cash flow due to prepayments and withdrawals.[14] Transactions costs also must be considered.

Duration Gap

Duration can be used to measure the interest rate sensitivity of any series of cash flows, such as from bonds and mortgages. In addition, duration can be used to measure a bank's interest rate sensitivity gap, which is called a *duration gap*. The basic idea of duration/immunization is to manage the gap between the duration of assets and liabilities to meet the goals of the bank. Suppose that the duration of the bank's assets is 360 days and the duration of its liabilities is 90 days, resulting in a gap of 270 days. The longer duration of the assets means that a given change in interest rates will change the present value of the assets more than the present value of the liabilities. The changed values of the assets and liabilities affects the market value of the bank's equity.

The following simplified example illustrates the change in equity.[15] The appendix at the end of this chapter shows an equation that may be used to compute the change in equity. In this example, a bank makes a single-payment loan with a face of $1,000, to be repaid in 360 days at an interest rate of 10 percent. Ten percent is the bank's opportunity cost. The present value of that loan (the dollar amount that the bank will extend to the borrower at the beginning of the year) is $909.09 ($1,000/1.10 = $909.09). To fund the loan, the bank borrows $909.09 at 8 percent every 90 days. The total cost to the bank for funding the loan for one year is \$981.82 (\$909.09 × 1.08 = \$981.82). The present value of the liability is \$892.56 (\$981.82/1.10 = \$892.56). Equity is the difference between the value of the bank's assets and liabilities. Thus, the value of the bank's equity is \$16.53.

Present Value of Assets and Liabilities
Assets	\$909.09
Liabilities	−892.56
Equity	\$ 16.53

If there is an unexpected 200 basis points increase in interest rates in 90 days, the present value of the assets will decline to \$892.86 (\$1,000/1.12 = \$892.86). The dollar amount of the liabilities will increase to \$995.42 due to the higher funding costs.[16] The present value of the \$995.42 is \$888.77 (\$995.42/1.12 = \$888.77). Accordingly, the value of the equity is \$4.09 (\$892.86 − \$888.77 = \$4.09). The 200 basis point increase in interest rates resulted in a decline of \$12.44 in the market value of the bank's equity—a 75.26 percent reduction!

Present Value of Assets and Liabilities
Assets	\$892.86
Liabilities	−887.77
Equity	\$ 4.09

The volatility of the equity is due to the mismatch between the duration of the assets and liabilities. If the duration of the assets and liabilities were the same, a 200 basis point increase in interest rates would have caused the value of the equity to fall \$0.30, only a 1.8 percent decline. Stated otherwise, *interest rate risk can be eliminated or immunized by setting the duration gap equal to zero.* Nevertheless, the elimination of interest rate risk is not always the best policy. Some banks prefer to manage their gaps to take advantage of expected changes in interest rates, rather than eliminate all interest rate risk.

Another advantage of using duration is that it can be used to gauge the effect of interest rate risk on equity. However, the market value of a bank's equity, determined by the difference between the duration of its assets and liabilities, should not to be confused with the stock market value of a bank. The stock market value of the bank takes factors other than duration of assets and liabilities into account. These factors include the payment of cash dividends, expectations about earnings, franchise value, and other considerations.

Next, the duration gap is a single number that takes into account both the timing and the magnitude of cash flows; it avoids the problems associated with arbitrary maturity buckets.

Finally, investment managers may use derivative securities, such as futures contracts and swaps, to alter their duration gaps.[17]

Simulations

Simulations are computer-generated scenarios about the future, which permit banks to analyze interest rate risk and business strategies in a dynamic framework. Given such information, banks may evaluate the desirability of various courses of action. The scenarios are based on a number of assumptions, such as the following:

- expected changes and levels of interest rates, and the shape of yield curves
- pricing strategies for assets and liabilities
- the growth, volume and mix of assets and liabilities
- hedging strategies

The data used for modeling the scenarios may include both historical data and "what if" projections.

The output of simulations can take a variety of forms, depending on the user's needs. Simulations can provide current and expected periodic gaps, duration gaps, balance sheet and income statements, performance measures, budgets, and financial reports. They can provide information about "macro hedges" (the entire balance sheet) or "micro hedges," (specific assets/liabilities). The information can be presented in tabular or graphic form. They can be simple, or "state-of-the-art." You can get whatever you want if you are willing to pay for it. The price of simulators ranges from a few thousand dollars to hundreds of thousands of dollars, depending on the degree of sophistication and service/infomation provided.

The principal advantage of simulations for interest rate risk management is that they are dynamic or forward looking. The accuracy of the simulations depends on the structure of the model and validity of the assumptions. If the structure or assumptions are wrong, inconsistent, or inappropriate for the bank using them, the output may result in inferior decisions by bank managers. Some simulation models use historic data and econometric techniques to estimate the parameters of structural equations used in the model. If the historic patterns are no longer valid, the equations will be misspecified, and the simulations will give misleading results. Similarly, suppose that a simulation forecasts quarterly net income, while interest rates are allowed to change more often. Changes in interest rates during the quarter may hide risks that are not revealed in the projected gap or net income at the end of the period. If managers were aware of the interim risks, they might choose different courses of action. This type of risk of using simulations and gap analysis is illustrated in Figure 3.1. It shows a bank's 0-90 day maturity bucket. Rate sensitive assets are a six-month, floating rate loan. Rate sensitive liabilities are an 8 percent CD with 90 days to maturity. The gap is zero. During the 90-day period, market interest rates decline sharply, resulting in interest rate risk that was not revealed by the gap analysis. Despite these shortcomings, the advantages of simulations outweigh the disadvantages. No interest rate risk management tool is perfect. So caveat emptor.

Figure 3.1   **Measurement Error**

0–90 Day Maturity Bucket

RSA $ 100
RSL   – 100
Gap   =   0
RSA   = 6 month, floating rate loan
RSL   = 8 percent CD with 90 days to maturity

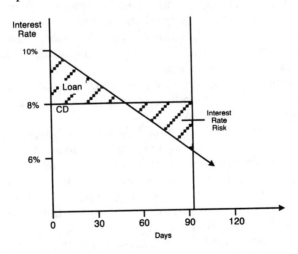

Endnotes

1. "How Chase Manhattan Manages Its Interest Rate Risk," *Financial Management Collection* (Fall 1988) Vol. 3, No. 3, 12–13.

2. Annual reports from 1987-1989 reveal the longer-term positive gaps offsetting the shorter-term negative gaps.

3. James E. McNulty, "Measuring Interest Rate Risk: What Do We Know?" *Journal of Retail Banking* (Spring-Summer 1986) 49-58; George Kaufman, "Measuring and Managing Interest Rate Risk: A Primer," *Economic Perspectives*, Federal Reserve Bank of Chicago (January-February, 1984) 16-29; Alden Toevs, "Gap Management: Managing Interest Rate Risk in Banks and Thrifts," *Economic Review*, Federal Reserve Bank of San Francisco (Spring 1983). Canada Deposit Insurance Corporation, *Interest Rate Risk Management*, No date, circa 1990.

4. Sherrill Schaffer, "Interest Rate Risk: What's a Bank to Do?" *Business Review*, Federal Reserve Bank of Philadelphia (May-June 1991) 17-27.

5. Federick R. Macaulay, *The Movements of Interest Rates, Bond Yields and Stock Prices in the United States Since 1856* (New York: National Bureau of Economic Research, 1938).

6. Several representative works on duration are: Gerald O. Bierwag, George G. Kaufman, and Alden L. Toevs, eds., *Innovations in Portfolio Management: Duration Analysis and Immunization* (Greenwich, CT.: JAI Press, 1983); Gerald O. Bierwag, *Duration Analysis: Managing Interest Rate Risk* (Cambridge, Mass.: Ballinger Publishing Co., 1987); Alden L. Toevs and William C. Haney, *Measuring and Managing Interest Rate Risk: A Guide to Asset/Liability Models Used in Banks and Thrifts* (New York: Morgan Stanley, 1984).

7. The duration of 10.92 differs from the amount shown in Table 3.2 because of different market yields.

8. This version of duration is commonly called "modified duration."

9. For information on convexity, see *Understanding Duration and Convexity* (Chicago: Chicago Board of Trade/Concepts and Applications, 1990); Frank J. Fabozzi and T. Dessa Fabozzi, *Bond Markets, Analysis and Strategies* (Englewood Cliffs, NJ.: Prentice Hall, 1989).

10. Lawrence Fisher and Roman Weil, "Coping With the Risk of Investment Rate Fluctuations: Return to Bondholders from Naive and Optimal Strategies," *Journal of Business* (October 1971) 408-431.

11. Bierwag, Kaufman, Schwitzer, and Toevs, "The Art of Risk Management." *Journal of Portfolio Management* (Spring 1981) 27-36.

12. This example is based on one that appears in Alfred Weinberger, Henry Nothof, and Kenneth Scott, *Duration Tables for Bond and Mortgage Portfolio Management* (Boston: Financial Publishing Co., 1980).

13. The $4,564 invested today at 8 percent, compounded semiannually, will provide $10,000 at the end of ten years. $(1 + .08/2)^{10 \times 2} = (1.04)^{20} = 2.1911$, $\$10,000/2.1911 = \$4,564$.

14. Martin L. Leibowitz, "Duration and Immunization: Matched-Funding Techniques," *Handbook of Financial Markets and Institutions*, 6th ed., Edward I. Altman, ed. (New York: John Wiley & Sons, 1987) Chapter 25; *Pros & Cons of Immunization: Proceedings of a Seminar on the Roles and Limits of Bond Immunization*, Martin L. Leibowitz, ed. (New York: Salomon Brothers, 1980).

15. Michael T. Belongia and G. J. Santoni, "Hedging Interest Rate Risk with Financial Futures: Some Basic Principles," *Review*, Federal Reserve Bank of St. Louis (October 1984) 15-25; also see George G. Kaufman, "Measuring and Managing Interest Rate Risk: A Primer," *Economic Perspectives*, Federal Reserve Bank of Chicago (January/Febuary 1984) 16-29; and Alden L. Toevs and William C. Haney, *Measuring and Managing Interest Rate Risk*, (New York: Morgan Stanley, 1984).

16. At the end of 90 days the liability is $926.75 ($909.09(1.08)^{.25}$). Then interest rates increase 200 basis points, and at the end of the year, the liability is $995.42 ($926.75(1.10)^{.75}$).

17. Gerald O. Bierwag and George G. Kaufman, "Duration Gaps with Futures and Swaps for Managing Interest Rate Risk at Depository Institutions," Unpublished paper (September 23, 1991).

Appendix 3

Calculating Duration and Equity Duration

Duration is the weighted average time to receive all cash flows (interest, dividends, and principal) where the weights reflect the relative present values of the cash flows. Although the concept is usually applied to debt securities, it may also be applied to stocks. However, we shall focus on the duration of bonds. The correct expression for duration depends on the assumed stochastic process driving interest rate movements. A flat term structure is assumed here.

$$D = \frac{\sum_{t=1}^{n} \left[\frac{C}{(1+i)^t} \right] t + \left[\frac{V}{(1+i)^n} \right] n}{\sum_{t=1}^{n} \left[\frac{C}{(1+i)^t} \right] + \left[\frac{V}{(1+i)^n} \right]} \qquad (3A\text{--}1)$$

where

D	= duration
C	= annual income expressed in dollars
V	= value of obligation at maturity
i	= interest rate per period

Alternately, the equation can be expressed as:

$$D = \frac{\sum_{t=1}^{n}\left[\dfrac{C}{(1+i)^t}\right]t + \left[\dfrac{V}{(1+i)^n}\right]n}{P_0}$$

(3A–2)

where

P_0 = the price of the bond

In fact, the denominator is the current market price of a bond. The numerator uses the same equation, but weights the present value of the cash flows by their time (years) to receipt. To illustrate the use of this equation, assume that a bond has a $1,000 face value, the coupon interest rate is 12 percent (it pays $120 interest) and the term to maturity is five years. If the current market rate of interest is 12 percent, the duration of the bond is four years, one year less than the term to maturity. The calculations are shown in Table 3A.1. The cash flows from the bond (column 2) were discounted by 12 percent and summed (column 4) to determine the market price of the bond. The market price is $1,000 because the 12 percent coupon bond was discounted by 12 percent, which is assumed to be the current market rate of interest. If the current market rate of interest were 14 percent, for example, the price of the bond would be $929.80.

Column 5 shows the present values of the cash flows as a percentage of the price that was determined in column 4. Finally, those values are weighted by the number of years listed in column 1. The sum of the values is the duration—4 years. If the coupons are paid twice a year, the duration is 3.90 years.

Equity Duration[1]

The dollar change in the market value of equity, and the duration of equity may be computed from the following equations. The duration of equity is interpreted in the same manner as the duration of a bond. That is, the longer the duration, the more interest rate sensitive the equity (bond).

$$DMV_e = \left[\frac{MV_1 \times D_1}{(1+i)} - \frac{MV_a \times D_a}{(1+i)}\right] \times \Delta i$$

(3A-3)

where

DMV_e = dollar change in the market value of equity

MV_1 = market value of liabilities

Table 3A.1   **Duration of 12 Percent Bond with 5 Years to Maturity Assuming a 12 Percent Market Yield**

Year	Cash Flow	PV Interest Factor @ 12%	PV of Cash Flow	PV of Cash Flow as % of Price ($1,000)	Weighted Values
1	2	3	4 = 2 × 3	5	6 = 1 × 5
1	$ 120	0.8929	$ 107.148	0.1071	0.1071
2	120	0.7972	95.664	0.0957	0.1914
3	120	0.7118	85.416	0.0854	0.2562
4	120	0.6355	76.260	0.0763	0.3050
5	$1,120	0.5674	635.488	0.6355	0.1774
			$1,000.000	1.0000	4.0371
			Price		Duration

When semiannual compounding is used, duration is 3.90 years.
Numbers may not add to totals due to rounding.

MV_a = market value of assets
D_l = duration of liabilities
D_a = duration of assets
Δi = change in interest rates

The equation implies that the duration of equity D_e is:

$$D_e = \frac{MV_a\, D_a - MV_l D_l}{MV_e}$$

Endnotes

1. The equations are from Alden L. Toevs and William C. Haney, *Measuring and Managing Interest Rate Risk* (New York: Morgan Stanley, 1984) 52.

CHAPTER 4

AN INTRODUCTION TO FORWARD RATE AGREEMENTS AND FUTURES

In this chapter we examine two similar hedging instruments: forward rate agreements and futures contracts. In later chapters we examine the roles that these instruments play in controlling interest rate risk.

Forward Rate Agreements

Terminology

A *forward contract* is. a contract between a buyer and a seller to trade something in the future at a price negotiated today. A forward contract is obligatory to both the buyer and the seller. For example, a forward contract to buy $1,000,000 par value of Treasury bills at a 6 percent discount rate in six months obligates the buyer to purchase the bills at a 6 percent discount rate, and it obligates the seller to sell the bills at the same price. If bills are selling for a 7 percent discount rate when the contract matures in six months, then the seller must sell bills and the buyer is obligated to purchase them at 6 percent, despite the fact that better rates/prices are available in the market.

There is a wide range of actively traded forward contracts available in interest rates, currencies, and energy products.

Forward rate agreements (FRAs) originated in Switzerland in 1984.[1] An FRA is a forward contract on interest rates. The buyers and sellers involved in FRAs are referred to as *counterparties*. One counterparty to the FRA will receive a fixed interest payment and pay a floating interest payment. This counterparty is referred to as the *receive fixed counterparty*. Figure 4.1 illustrates the relevant time periods and cash flows for the receive fixed counterparty. The fixed interest payment is set on the *signing date* when the contract is initiated. Typically, there are no cash flows on the signing date.

The *floating interest payment* is set on the *reset date*, which is specified in the FRA. We let "s" denote the number of days between the

Figure 4.1   Time Frame and Cash Flows of a Receive Fixed,
               Pay Floating FRA

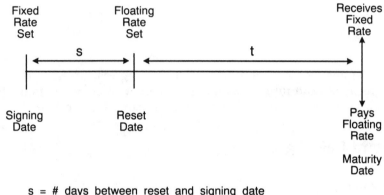

s = # days between reset and signing date
t = # days between maturity and reset date

signing date and the reset date. The reset date is different from the sign-ing date. Interest accrues between the reset date and the maturity date. We let "t" denote the number of days between the reset date and the contract *maturity date* of the contract. In review, the fixed rate payment is determined on the signing date; the floating rate payment is deter-mined on the reset date.

The other counterparty to the FRA, who will receive a floating in-terest payment and pay a fixed interest payment, is referred to as the *receive floating counterparty*. In an FRA, the receive fixed counterparty agrees to make a floating interest payment to the receive floating coun-terparty in exchange for receiving a fixed interest payment. The fixed and floating payments are based on (1) the specified notional principal, (2) an acceptable interest rate measure, and (3) the specified time frame.

First, the *notional principal* is the amount on which interest is paid. The notional principal is not actually paid, rather the FRA is cash set-tled. *Cash settled* refers to the payment of the difference between the contract rate agreed upon (that is, the fixed rate) and the prevailing market rate. Most FRAs are *advanced settled*, meaning cash payments are made on the reset date. However, some FRAs are *settled in arrears*, which means the cash payment is made on the contract maturity date. In any case, only the net cash flow is exchanged.

Second, LIBOR (London Interbank Offer Rate) is the typical interest rate measure. However, the interest rate measure could be the Federal funds rate, the 90-day Treasury bill rate, the prime rate, or some other rate. The interest rate measure determines how the interest rate is compounded as well as determining the floating rate on the reset date. For example, the interest rate measure could be based on a 360-day year (LIBOR and Treasury bills) or a 365-day year (Treasury notes and bonds).

Third, the specified time frame includes the time between the signing date and the reset date(s) as well as the time between the reset date and the contract maturity date(s). FRAs are quoted as "in three, for six" which means the reset date is in three months, and the contract maturity date is six months after the reset date. The total time frame is nine months. These months are typically actual calendar months, not 30 days.

FRAs contain *counterparty risk*. Counterparty risk is the risk that the party on the opposite side of the contract might default. This is why FRA contracts are advanced settled. Advanced settled refers to making the interest payments within the FRA on the reset date where the payment amounts have been appropriately discounted from the maturity date to the reset date.[2] To minimize default risk, counterparties frequently exchange collateral. That is, each counterparty gives collateral to the other counterparty as surety to perform on the contract. For example, a bank could give some Treasury securities as collateral for the FRA. FRAs can be custom designed to meet an institution's unique needs.

Illustration of Receive Fixed and Pay Floating

Let's examine the cash flow related to the counterparty who receives the fixed interest payment and pays floating. We assume the contract is settled in arrears (payments are made on the maturity date), which simplifies the issues. That is, the contract is not advanced settled.

For purposes of illustration, we use an "in two, for three" FRA on LIBOR for $1 million notional principal. The reset date is in 60 days (assuming for simplicity the months have 30 days each) and the maturity date is 90 days after the reset date. We let "N(t)" denote the notional principal from which we calculate the interest accrual over t. Hence, s = 60, t = 90, and N(t) = $1,000,000.

LIBOR is quoted on a *money market yield* basis (which is also known as an *add-on rate*). Add-on rates assume that the interest is "added on" the notional principal amount. Specifically,

$$\text{Payments} = N(t) + \left[\frac{\text{Rate}(\%)}{100}\right]\left[\frac{\text{Days}}{360}\right]N(t) \qquad (4\text{--}1)$$

where Payment is the amount owed to pay off the loan, $N(t)$ is the notional principal, Rate is the quoted add-on rate (in percent), and Days is the number of days the loan is held. The amount on the right side of the plus sign is the interest payment.

Suppose the current LIBOR forward rate for an "in two, for three" is 7.0 percent (denote "fx(t)," fx(t) = 7.0). The fixed rate payment on this FRA at maturity will be:

$$R_{fx}(t) = \left[\frac{fx(t)}{100}\right]\left[\frac{t}{360}\right]N(t) \qquad (4\text{--}2)$$

which is the interest rate times the fraction of the "year" held, times the loan amount or notional principal. In our example, we have:

$$R_{fx}(t) = \left[\frac{7.0}{100}\right]\left[\frac{90}{360}\right]\$1,000,000$$

$$R_{fx}(t) = \$17,500$$

The receive fixed counterparty will receive \$17,500 in five months (two months to the reset date and three months from there to the contract maturity date). Figure 4.2 highlights the cash flows for the receive fixed counterparty. However, this counterparty will have to make a payment based on the floating rate that is determined on the reset date.

Figure 4.2   **Cash Flows for an In Two, For Three Receive Fixed FRA**

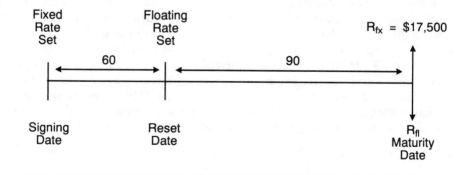

The magnitude of the net cash flow is a function of the floating rate determined on the reset date. If rates fall, then the net cash flow rises.

If three-month LIBOR is below 7.0 percent on the reset date, then the receive fixed counterparty will profit. Suppose that interest rates fall, and three-month LIBOR on the reset date is 6.9 percent. We denote this floating rate as fl(t). The dollar floating rate payment is:

$$R_{fl}(t) = \left[\frac{fl(t)}{100}\right]\left[\frac{t}{360}\right]N(t) \qquad (4\text{--}3)$$

$$R_{fl}(t) = \left[\frac{6.9}{100}\right]\left[\frac{90}{360}\right]1{,}000{,}000$$

$$R_{fl}(t) = \$17{,}250$$

Because FRAs are settled with a net cash payment, the receive fixed counterparty will receive \$250 ($R_{fx}(t) - R_{fl}(t) = \$17{,}500 - \$17{,}250$) from the receive floating counterparty on the maturity date.[3]

Figure 4.3 shows the *payoff diagram* for this "in two, for three" FRA to the receive fixed counterparty. A payoff diagram maps the dollar profit and loss from a security at one point of time, the maturity date. LIBOR is on the horizontal axis. In our case the variable is the three-month LIBOR denoted "fl(t)." From equation (4–3) we see that one *basis point* (one percent of one percent) is worth \$25.

$$R_{fl}(t) = \left[\frac{0.01}{100}\right]\left[\frac{90}{360}\right]1{,}000{,}000 = \$25$$

The value of a basis point is a function of the days to maturity and the notional principal amount. In Figure 4–3, we see that if rates fall from 7 percent to 5 percent—a 200 basis point drop—then the FRA will be worth \$5,000 (200*\$25). Therefore, for every one basis point drop in rates, the FRA gains \$25. Similarly, for every one basis point rise in rates, the FRA loses \$25.

The payoff diagram for the receive floating counterparty is the mirror image of the receive fixed counterparty. Figure 4.4 shows this relationship. FRAs are a zero sum game, which means that for every dollar the receive fixed counterparty makes, the receive floating counterparty has lost a dollar.

The following examples illustrate the advantages and disadvantages of using FRAs in asset/liability management. The framework is a simplification, but the general inferences are the same. We employ the principle of value additivity in this simple case, as well as in the more general cases.

Figure 4.3   **Payoff Diagram for In Two, For Three FRA (Fixed)**

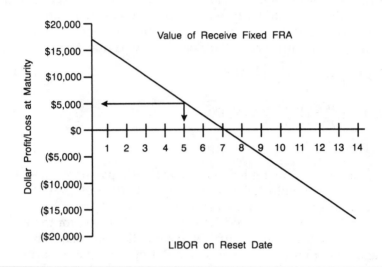

Figure 4.4   **Payoff Diagram for In Two, For Three FRA (Floating)**

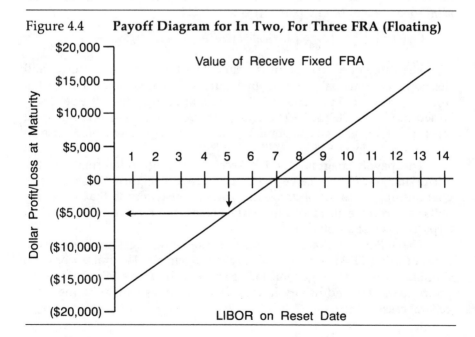

Box 4.1   Financial Engineering via Building Blocks

Value additivity is a widely accepted principle applied throughout the field of finance. Value additivity means the sum of the parts is equal to the whole. For example, a portfolio of securities is worth the sum of each individual security's value. By combining securities in various elegant ways, we neither add to nor subtract from the portfolio value, which remains merely additive. We can value an institution's security portfolio as the sum of the individual securities.

With the principle of value additivity, you can comprehend the characteristics of a portfolio by examining the portfolio's individual securities. If each security is considered a building block and the portfolio is considered a building, then the building can be understood by examining the underlying blocks. Hence, the term *building blocks* is applied. You can build portfolios with various building blocks, such as forward rate agreements, futures, options, swaps, and so forth. In this regard, value additivity is appropriately used for assessing the cost of hedging and its impact on an institution's net interest income and its value.

Value additivity is *not* appropriate for valuing institutions as a whole for the following reasons. First, there is more to a financial institution than security holdings. Institutions generate fee income, such as mortgage servicing, trust accounts, and so forth. Second, institutions have franchise value or goodwill. Third, the unique characteristics of the institution's equity value cannot be acquired elsewhere. If an institution has equity with highly desirable characteristics, such as minimal adverse interest rate risk, then the market value of the equity will be driven up by investor demand. Thus, a financial institution's value is decisively different from actively traded securities in its portfolio. An investor cannot "create" a portfolio which mimics the institution's specific attributes.

Example 1: Invest in Two Months LIBOR for Three Months.

Suppose you are the manager of a small bank in Texas which will receive a $1,000,000 payment in two months. Also, contractually your institution has agreed to lend $1,017,000 in five months. Based on the current financial environment, you decide the best way to invest the $1 million is in a Euro-CD (LIBOR deposit). Your concern is that interest rates will fall over the next two months, reducing the interest earned on the deposit. Keep in mind that your institution is committed to make a $1,017,000 loan in five months. Figure 4.5a illustrates the cash flow from this pending Euro-CD deposit.

Under current market conditions you anticipate earning 7.0 percent on this deposit, which amounts to $17,500. If rates fall 50 basis points to 6.5 percent, this deposit will only earn:

$$R_{fl}(t) = \left[\frac{6.5}{100}\right]\left[\frac{90}{360}\right] 1,000,000 = \$16,250$$

an opportunity loss of $1,250. Thus, with just these proceeds, you will not be able to lend the $1,017,000.

To hedge this interest rate risk, enter an "in two, for three" receive fixed FRA. The fixed rate on the FRA is 7.0 percent. Figure 4.5b illustrates the pattern of cash flows for this FRA.

What is the result of having both a pending Euro-CD deposit and a receive fixed FRA? As shown in Figures 4.5a and 4.5b, the floating rate interest payment made on the deposit can be used to pay the floating side of the FRA. The only interest payment remaining is the receipt of the fixed interest payment on the FRA. Therefore, by combining a pending Euro-CD with an FRA we have produced a synthetic fixed rate deposit. Figure 4.5c illustrates the resulting cash flows from the portfolio of the Euro-CD and the FRA.

Several observations can be made from this example. First, the risk of falling interest rates has been eliminated: you will earn 7 percent. Second, the opportunity to earn higher rates has also been eliminated. For example, if rates rose to 10 percent you would still earn on net 7 percent (giving up $7,500 in potential interest). Figure 4.6 illustrates the opportunity gains and losses incurred under different interest rate changes. As interest rates rise, you will be disappointed that the FRA was employed because you will have to pay $R_{fl}(t) - R_{fx}(t)$ on the FRA. This is the cost of eliminating interest rate risk with FRAs.

Forward contracts are a two-edged sword. Interest rate risk can be totally eliminated; however, there is the possibility for an opportunity loss. In the example here, the opportunity loss is incurred when interest rates rise.

There are other important considerations, including counterparty risk and *quantity risk*. Quantity risk refers to the uncertainty surrounding whether the underlying deposit your institution expects to receive in 60 days will be made. Consider the following scenario: You anticipated the $1 million deposit and entered an FRA as a receive fixed counterparty. Now interest rates spike up to 10 percent, and the deposit

Figure 4.5a   **Cash Flows from Euro-CD Deposit**

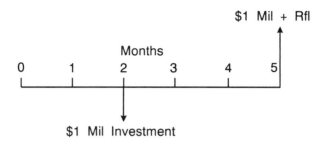

Figure 4.5b   **Cash Flows from a Receive Fixed FRA**

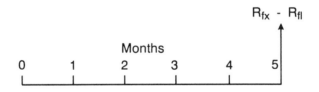

Figure 4.5c   **Cash Flows from Both the Deposit and FRA**

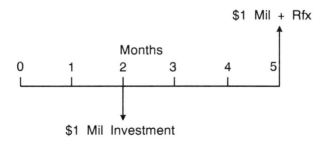

Figure 4.6   **Opportunity Gains and Losses of Receive Fixed FRA**

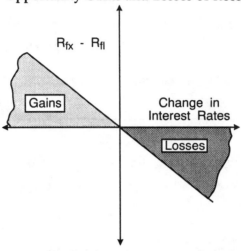

is not made for any number of reasons. By the maturity date there was
no deposit and you must pay on the FRA

$$R_{fl}(t) - R_{fx}(t) = \left[\frac{10.0}{100}\right]\left[\frac{90}{360}\right]1,000,000 - \left[\frac{7.0}{100}\right]\left[\frac{90}{360}\right]1,000,000$$

$$= \$7,500$$

Extreme caution is in order for hedging with FRAs where there is
large quantity risk. More will be said about this later. Let's consider a
second example.

Example 2: Borrow in Two Months LIBOR for Three Months.

Suppose your bank will borrow $1,000,000 in two months for three
months with a Eurodollar loan (borrowing based on LIBOR). You have
also contractually agreed to invest $1 million in a LIBOR investment
earning 7.5 percent in two months for three months. Figure 4.7a illustrates the cash flow from this pending loan.

Now, under current market conditions you anticipate paying 7
percent on the borrowed funds. Therefore, your interest payment on the
loan is anticipated to be $17,500. The interest earned on the LIBOR in-
vestment will be $18,750 (based on 7.5 percent interest rate). Hence, the
way the deal is now structured your bank should earn $1,750.

Figure 4.7a   Cash Flows for In Two, For Three Loan
(Up Arrow Implies Cash Inflow, Down Arrow Implies Cash Outflow)

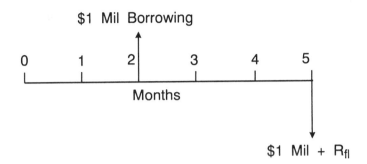

Figure 4.7b   In Two, For Three FRA (Receive Fixed)

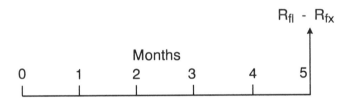

Figure 4.7c   In Two, For Three Loan and FRA

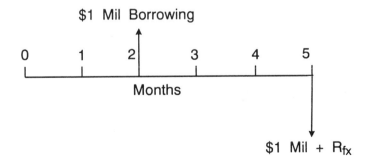

Clearly, the concern is that interest rates will rise over the next two months, increasing your interest payments on the loan and narrowing (or possibly eliminating) your net income. If interest rates rise above 7.5 percent, then this deal will be unprofitable. To hedge this interest rate risk, enter an "in two, for three" receive floating FRA. The fixed rate on the FRA is 7.0 percent. Figure 4.7b illustrates the cash flow from this receive floating FRA.

The result of having both a pending LIBOR loan and a receive floating FRA is fixed rate borrowing. To see this, look again at Figures 4.7a and 4.7b. Notice the floating interest payment on the loan can be paid by the floating interest receipt on the FRA. The only interest payment remaining is the fixed payment on the FRA. Therefore, by combining a pending loan with an FRA, we have produced a synthetic fixed rate loan. Figure 4.7c illustrates the resulting cash flows from the portfolio of the loan and the FRA.

Similar observations can be made from this example. First, the risk of rising rates has been eliminated: you will pay 7 percent for sure, and profit $1,250 for sure. Second, the opportunity to pay lower rates has also been eliminated. Figure 4.8 illustrates the opportunity gains and losses from employing the FRA.

Both counterparty risk and quantity risk are present here. As mentioned previously, both of these risks should be carefully examined before

---

Figure 4.8   **Opportunity Gains and Losses of Receive Floating**

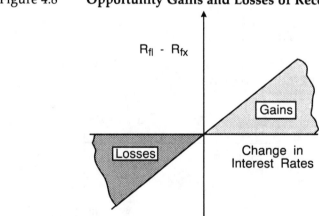

engaging in FRAs. Thus, through these examples, we have seen that FRAs are powerful tools to manage interest rate risk. Pending exposures to rate changes can be neutralized at the expense of forgoing future profit opportunities when rates move in your favor.

Futures Contracts

A *futures contract* is a marketable forward contract. A futures contract is an agreement to make delivery (short) at a later date, or to accept delivery (long) of a fixed amount of a specific quality of an asset at a specified price. (Cash settled contracts require the futures contract to be settled with cash payments rather than physical delivery.) Liquid futures markets in numerous commodities and securities, including interest rate contracts, now exist. LIBOR-based interest rate futures contracts were first introduced at the Chicago Mercantile Exchange with the Eurodollar contract in 1981. Currently, interest rate futures contracts include one- and three-month Eurodollars, Treasury bills, Treasury notes, and Treasury bonds.

Futures contracts require a *margin deposit* (or *performance bond*), which is a good faith deposit to guarantee performance on the contract, usually 0.5 percent to 10 percent of the contract value. The *settlement price* is an average of futures prices near the end of the day (not the closing price). Futures contracts are *marked-to-market*, which means profits and losses are taken daily, based on the change in settlement prices. While forwards contracts have profits taken at the expiration date of the contract, futures have profits taken each day. Therefore, futures contracts require daily monitoring because they may require sizable amounts of cash (sometimes within hours). These daily cash flow requirements result in slight pricing differences between FRAs and interest rate futures (called the *financing bias*).[4] Specifically, for Eurodollar futures which are quoted in "price" (100-LIBOR), the bias is in favor of the short side when compared to FRAs. If a Eurodollar futures is quoted as 94.50, then the implied LIBOR rate is 5.50 percent (100 − 94.50).

The *basis* refers to the spread between the cash price and the futures price, which may be positive, zero, or negative. Futures contracts contain no counterparty risk because the exchange stands as an intermediary. Futures contracts typically are liquid. One measure of liquidity is the amount of *open interest*.[5] Open interest is the number of futures contracts which exist at any point in time. For example, in late

1991 the 90-day Eurodollar futures contract had open interest in excess of one million contracts (each contract is for one million notional principal), which implies this contract is very liquid. Futures contracts have standardized terms and cannot be tailored to specific needs. Figure 4.9 illustrates the cash flows from a futures contract. We see from this figure that profits are taken daily. Losses are paid once the maintenance margin is "hit." Once the losses reduce the margin to the level of the maintenance margin, then the investor is required to post margin back up to the initial margin. Thus, the cash outflows are infrequent and large.

The examples for forward contracts remain basically the same for futures contracts with the exception of when cash flows are paid and received.

Forwards versus Futures

Forward contracts are expensive for firms with poor credit ratings because of the collateral required and the dealer mark-ups. Risky firms may have to post an enormous amount of collateral to enter a forward. Therefore, firms with a low credit rating will probably find futures preferable to FRAs. With futures, however, you could face a squeeze on cash flow and be forced out of a position at the very time you need to maintain the hedged position. For example, if you have purchased a Eurodollar futures contract and interest rates rise (and hence prices fall) you will have to post more margin. It is possible that at the very time more margin has to be posted, your firm is short on cash (due to the rise in interest rates). If cash margin cannot be posted, then the brokerage firm will sell your position at a severe loss.

Figure 4.9   **Cash Flows from a Futures Contract**

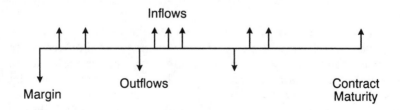

Summary

The focus of this chapter was introducing forward rate agreements (FRAs) and futures contracts, and their role in hedging interest rate risk. FRAs and futures are powerful tools in managing interest rate risk. These tools can be used to eliminate the impact of adverse moves in interest rates. Unfortunately, these tools will also eliminate the impact of positive interest rate moves.

We also introduced the notion of value additivity (the sum of the parts equals the whole) and its role in financial engineering. Value additivity is appropriate for examining the interest rate risk of a financial institution, but value additivity is not appropriate for trying to determine the market value of the firm. In the next chapter we examine more complex uses of futures for asset/liability management.

Endnotes

1. See Marcia L. Stigum, *The Money Market*, 3rd Edition (Homewood, IL: Dow Jones Irwin, 1990), page 875.

2. For the technical details of advanced settlement see Appendix 4A.

3. As will be discussed later, most FRAs are actually settled on the reset date by paying the present value of the difference.

4. For more details on the pricing biases see Appendix 4B.

5. Another measure of liquidity is volume.

Appendix 4A

Pricing LIBOR Forward Rate Agreements

The following is a brief technical description of FRAs for LIBOR contracts. These technical details are based on the British Bankers' Association procedures (denoted FRABBA and pronounced fraa-baa). Let:

$fx(t)$	= the fixed LIBOR rate quoted in the FRA
$fl(t)$	= the floating LIBOR market rate observed on the reset date (usually eight BBA quality banks surveyed at 11:00 A.M.)
t	= the number of days covering the FRA (the days between the reset date and the maturity date)
s	= the number of days until the reset date
$N(t)$	= the notional principal (amount "deposited" on the reset date)
S	= the amount of cash transferred on FRAs at the maturity date, the settle value
AS	= the amount of cash transferred on an advanced settled FRA

Recall LIBOR contracts are quoted on a money market yield basis and are calculated on a 360-day year. Hence, the future value of $1 "FV" invested at 10 percent for 90 days is worth the following:

$$FV = \$1 \left[1 + \frac{(10\%/100)\,90}{360} \right] = \$1.025$$

The FRA will pay the difference between the floating market rate and the specified-in-advance fixed contract rate on the maturity date. For a receive fixed and pay floating (FRA) the cash payment made on the maturity date is as follows:

$$S = N(t) [fl(t) - fx(t)] \left[\frac{t}{360} \right]$$

The advanced settle amount is just the cash payment at maturity discounted to the reset date.

$$AS = \left[\frac{S}{1 + \dfrac{fl(t)t}{360}} \right] = \left[\frac{NP [fx(t) - fl(t)] \left[\dfrac{t}{360} \right]}{1 + \left[\dfrac{fl(t)t}{360} \right]} \right]$$

The cash payments for a receive floating and pay fixed are just the opposite of the formula above. Hence, trading in FRAs is a zero sum game. For every dollar lost there is a dollar gain, ignoring trading costs.

Pricing FRAs

How are we to know whether the interest rate quoted in the FRA is reasonable? If we ignore trading costs, then the *law of one price* should prevail. The law of one price states that portfolios with identical future cash flows should trade at the same price today. Hence, we make the following observation. Consider investing one dollar in a short LIBOR contract at fx(s) and also investing in an FRA at fx(t). Alternatively, consider just investing one dollar in a long LIBOR contract at fx(s+t). Schematically, we illustrate these choices in Figure 4A.1.

Figure 4A.1   Time Frame and Interest Rates to Compute FRA

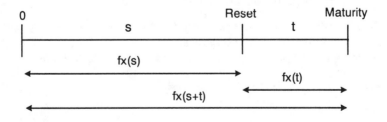

Numerically, one dollar invested in the short LIBOR (fx(s)) and an FRA will at maturity be worth:

$$\$1\left[1+\frac{fx(s)s}{360}\right]\left[1+\frac{fx(t)t}{360}\right]$$

and one dollar invested in just a long LIBOR will at maturity be worth:

$$\$1\left[1+\frac{fx(s+t)(s+t)}{360}\right]$$

The value of both of these investments at maturity should be the same. Thus,

$$\$1\left[1+\frac{fx(s)s}{360}\right]\left[1+\frac{fx(t)t}{360}\right]=\$1\left[1+\frac{fx(s+t)(s+t)}{360}\right]$$

Based on this equality, we can solve for the forward rate, fx(t), which makes the above equation correct. The equation for fx(t) is as follows:

$$fx(t)=\left[\frac{360}{t}\right]\left[\frac{1+\dfrac{fx(s+t)(s+t)}{360}}{1+\dfrac{fx(s)s}{360}}-1\right]$$

The above equation gives the equilibrium interest rate for a LIBOR FRA.

Appendix 4B

Pricing Interest Rate Futures Contracts

The pricing of interest rate futures contracts is the same as forward contracts with the exception of the financing bias. For short-term contracts (one year or less), this bias is relatively small. For longer-term contracts, the bias is significant. We adopt the following notation:

frafx(t)	= the FRA interest rate
fcfx(t)	= the interest rate implied by the futures contract
sd	= the volatility of forward interest rates (standard deviation)
t	= the number of days until the futures contract matures

The following is an ad hoc adjustment that is fairly accurate.[1] This adjustment is converting an interest rate implied by a futures contract into an interest rate implied by an FRA.

$$\text{frafx(t)} = \text{fcfx(t)}\exp\left[-\frac{1}{2}\,\text{sd}^2\,\text{fcfx(t)}\left(\frac{t}{365}\right)\right]$$

The term (t/365) is the fraction of the year and could easily be (t/360) if desired. This adjustment is just an estimate, but the main issue is to realize that there are subtle pricing differences. Thus, we see that interest rates implied by the futures contracts are slightly biased high. The bias is greater the larger the volatility of interest rates, the larger the level of rates, and the longer the contract life.

Endnotes

1. See Terry Belton and Galen Burghardt, "The Financing Bias in Eurodollar Futures Prices," Research Paper, Discount Corporation of New York Futures, Chicago, IL 60604 (March 22, 1990).

CHAPTER 5

HEDGING WITH
FINANCIAL FUTURES

Financial futures are futures contracts on financial instruments. Financial futures are similar to futures contracts on grains and metals, except that the underlying asset consists of Treasury securities, domestic Certificates of Deposit, Eurodollar time deposits, and other types of financial instruments, including stock and bond indexes. The first financial futures contract was the Government National Mortgage Association-Collateralized Depository Receipt (GNMA-CDR). GNMA-CDR contracts began trading on the Chicago Board of Trade (CBOT) in 1975. The following year, the International Monetary Market (IMM) division of the Chicago Mercantile Exchange introduced a futures contract on Treasury bills. Since then, the market for financial futures has virtually exploded with new contracts and large trading volumes.

Contract Specifications

Financial futures contracts specify the trading units, delivery grades of the underlying asset being traded, and other features. The CBOT contract specifications for Treasury bond futures contracts are presented in Table 5.1. The trading unit is one U.S. Treasury bond having a face value at maturity of $100,000. Our initial focus is on the delivery grade of U.S. Treasury bonds, which is then used to illustrate some key aspects of dealing in Treasury futures.

The delivery grade varies from one financial commodity to another. For example, the delivery grade for three-month Treasury bill futures is U.S. Treasury bills with 13 weeks to maturity. The delivery grade for Eurodollar Time Deposit futures is cash settlement with the Chicago Mercantile Exchange Clearinghouse. The rest of the table is self-explanatory.

Table 5.1   **U.S. Treasury Bond Futures Contract Specifications**
Trading Unit
   One U.S. Treasury bond having a face value at maturity of
   $100,000 or multiples thereof
Deliverable Grade
   U.S. Treasury bonds that, if callable, are not callable for at least
   15 years from the first day of the delivery month or, if not
   callable, have a maturity of at least 15 years from the first
   business day of the delivery month. The invoice price equals
   the futures settlement price times a conversion factor, plus
   accrued interest. The conversion factor is the price of the
   delivered bond ($1 par value) to yield 8 percent.
Price Quotation
   Points ($1,000) and thirty-seconds of a point; for example, 80-16
   equals 80 16/32
Tick Size
   One thirty-second (1/32) of a point ($31.25 per contract); par is
   on the basis of 100 points.
Daily Price Limit
   3 points ($3000 per contract) above or below the previous day's
   settlement price (expandable to 4 1/2 points). Limits are lifted
   the second business day preceding the first day of the
   delivery month.
Contract Months
   March, June, September, and December
Delivery Method
   Federal Reserve book-entry wire transfer system
Last Trading Day
   Seventh business day preceding the last business day of the
   delivery month
Last Delivery Day
   Last business day of the delivery month
Trading Hours
   7:20 A.M. to 2:00 P.M. (Chicago time), Monday through Friday.
   Evening trading hours are 5:00 to 8:30 P.M. (central standard
   time) or 6:00 to 9:30 P.M. (central daylight saving time),
   Sunday through Thursday. On the last trading day of an
   expiring contract, trading in that contract stops at noon.
Ticker Symbol
   US
Source: Chicago Board of Trade, Contract Specifications, 1991, p. 55.

CBOT Treasury bond and note futures contracts specify the delivery of "nominally" 8 percent coupon financial instruments. In the case of Treasury bond futures contracts, the contract allows delivery of any U.S. Treasury bond with at least 15 years to maturity if not callable and, if callable, at least 15 years to maturity from the first day of the delivery month. As shown in Table 5.2, there were 24 Treasury bond issues eligible for delivery in January 1992. Consequently, the CBOT has developed *conversion factors* (CF) to adjust the principal invoice prices (price excluding accrued interest) of those bonds with different maturities and coupons so that they meet the nominal 8 percent standard for a hypothetical bond with 20 years to maturity. Bonds with coupons in excess of 8 percent have a CF greater than one. Bonds with coupons of less than 8 percent have a CF of less than one. Those with coupons equal to 8 percent have a CF equal to one. By way of illustration, a 12 percent bond with 25 years to maturity has a CF of 1.4296. A CF of 1.4296 means that bond is worth about 143 percent of an 8 percent bond with 20 years to maturity—the standard used for the conversion factors. A 10 percent bond with 15 years to maturity has a CF of 1.1729. This bond is worth about 117 percent of an 8 percent bond with 20 years to maturity (See Table 5.3).

Cheapest-to-Deliver

The CFs are used to determine the principal invoice price of interest rate futures contracts. The principal invoice price plus accrued interest is the total invoice price of the contract.

Principal invoice = Futures settlement × $1,000 × CF   (5-1)

For example, June '94 futures contracts settle at 98-00 and the CF is 1.4296 for a 12 percent bond with 25 years to maturity. The principal invoice price is $140,100.80 (98 × $1,000 × 1.4296). Similarly, the principal invoice price of the 10 percent bond with 15 years to maturity is $114,944.20 (98 × $1,000 × 1.1729).

As a result of variation in prices among deliverable bonds, sellers select for delivery the cash instrument that has the lowest cash price (including accrued interest and cost of carry or financing), which is known as the *cheapest-to-deliver* (CTD).[1] If the 10 percent and 12 percent bonds in the previous example were the only two available for delivery, sellers would select the 10 percent bond because of the lower principal invoice price.

Table 5.2   U.S. Treasury Bond Futures Contract Conversion Factors

Coupon	Maturity	Amount ($Blns)	Mar 92	Jun 92	Sep 92	Dec 92	Mar 93	Jun 93
1. 7-1/4	May 15, 2016	18.82	0.9205	0.9206	0.9211	0.9212	0.9217	0.9218
2. 7-1/2	Nov 15, 2016	18.86	0.9466	0.9466	0.9470	0.9470	0.9474	0.9474
3. 7-7/8	Feb 15, 2021	11.01	0.9858	0.9860	0.9859	0.9861	0.9860	0.9862
4. 8*	Nov 15, 2021	12.01	1.0000	0.9998	1.0000	0.9998	1.0000	0.9998
5. 8-1/8	May 15, 2021	11.75	1.0140	1.0138	1.0140	1.0137	1.0139	1.0137
6. 8-1/8	Aug 15, 2021	12.01	1.0139	1.0140	1.0138	1.0140	1.0137	1.0139
7. 8-1/8	Aug 15, 2019	20.01	1.0136	1.0137	1.0135	1.0137	1.0134	1.0136
8. 8-1/2	Feb 15, 2020	10.06	1.0552	1.0553	1.0549	1.0550	1.0546	1.0547
9. 8-3/4	May 15, 2017	18.19	1.0806	1.0801	1.0800	1.0795	1.0795	1.0790
10. 8-3/4	May 15, 2020	10.01	1.0833	1.0829	1.0829	1.0825	1.0825	1.0820
11. 8-3/4	Aug 15, 2020	21.01	1.0833	1.0833	1.0829	1.0829	1.0825	1.0825
12. 8-7/8	Aug 15, 2017	14.02	1.0941	1.0940	1.0935	1.0934	1.0928	1.0927

*Most recently auctioned 30-yr. T-bond eligible for delivery

Table 5.2   U.S. Treasury Bond Futures Contract Conversion Factors (continued)

Coupon	Maturity	Amount ($Blns)	Mar 92	Jun 92	Sep 92	Dec 92	Mar 92	Jun 92
13. 8-7/8	Feb 15, 2019	19.25	1.0957	1.0957	1.0952	1.0951	1.0946	1.0946
14. 9	Nov 15, 2018	9.03	1.1094	1.1088	1.1087	1.1082	1.1081	1.1075
15. 9-1/8	May 15, 2018	8.71	1.1223	1.1217	1.1216	1.1210	1.1208	1.1202
16. 9-1/4	Feb 15, 2016	7.27	1.1318	1.1315	1.1308	1.1305	1.1298	1.1295
17. 9-7/8	Nov 15, 2015	6.90	1.1973	1.1963	1.1958	1.1948	1.1943	1.1932
18. 10-3/8	Nov 15, 2007-12	11.03	1.2089	1.2069	1.2053	—	—	—
19. 10-5/8	Aug 15, 2015	7.15	1.2749	1.2741	1.2728	1.2720	1.2706	—
20. 11-1/4	Feb 15, 2015	12.67	1.3378	1.3367	1.3350	1.3339	1.3322	—
21. 11-3/4	Nov 15, 2009-14	6.01	1.3500	1.3473	1.3452	1.3425	1.3403	1.3374
22. 12	Aug 15, 2008-13	14.76	1.3599	1.3575	1.3544	1.3518	1.3485	1.3458
23. 12-1/2	Aug 15, 2009-14	5.13	1.4168	1.4143	1.4110	1.4083	1.4050	1.4022
24. 13-1/4	May 15, 2009-14	5.01	1.4833	1.4795	1.4764	1.4725	1.4692	1.4652

Total eligible for delivery $290.68 billion
Source: CBOT

Table 5.3	Selected Treasury Bond Conversion Factors to Yield 8 Percent			
	Coupon Rates			
Years	8%	10%	12%	14%
15	1.0000	1.1729	1.3438	1.5188
20	1.0000	1.1979	1.3959	1.5938
25	1.0000	1.2148	1.4296	1.6445

The security that is CTD changes over time. One reason for the change is because of the volatility of market rates of interest. When market yields are greater than 8 percent, the CF system tends to favor low coupon, long-term bonds. When yields are less than 8 percent, the CF system favors high coupon, short-term bonds. Another reason is that some investors prefer discount over premium securities for tax reasons. Finally, the shape of the yield curve is a consideration in determining which security is the CTD.

The price of interest rate futures contracts tends to track the price of the CTD.[2] The difference between the price of the futures contract and the CTD is called the *basis*. The amount of basis depends on short-term financing rates, the yield of the cash security, and the time remaining to maturity of the contract. The basis should approach zero during the delivery month because sellers may make delivery any day during that month. Most hedgers close out their positions before the contract delivery date. Therefore, trading futures contracts during the delivery month usually means trading the CTD security.

The Basics of Hedging

The traditional function of the futures market is to shift the risk of price changes of commodities from those who do not want it (hedgers) to those who do want it for a price (speculators). In addition to the traditional function, the futures market is used by profit maximizing firms to enhance their incomes. As will be explained later in this chapter, buying and selling futures contracts acts as a temporary substitute for cash market transactions. Futures contracts may be used to alter the effective maturity (lengthen or shorten) of a fixed-income portfolio. Futures contracts may be used to create "synthetic" financial instruments. Finally, futures contracts are more liquid than cash securities, and transaction costs are relatively low in the futures market.[3]

Interest rate futures are quoted in terms of prices rather than in terms of interest rates or yields. If market rates of interest increase, the price of interest rate futures contracts declines, and vice versa. To hedge against falling prices (rising rates), you would sell interest rate futures contracts short. A *short sale* is the sale of futures contracts (cash commodity, or security) without taking the offsetting action of buying contracts. A speculator who sells short sells futures contracts at a high price in anticipation of buying them back at a lower price. A hedger who sells short accepts price movements in either direction. The difference between the high selling price and the lower purchase price is profit. If the price goes up, instead of going down, a loss is incurred.

To hedge against higher prices (falling rates) you would buy (go long) interest rate futures contracts. The terms *cash market* and *spot market* are industry jargon for trades in commodities for immediate (the same or next business day) delivery. A cash market position refers to the physical commodity (security) as distinguished from the futures commodity. The cash price is the price now. A futures position refers to transactions in the futures market.

Minimum Variance Hedge

The following examples demonstrate how risk-avoiding hedgers use interest rate futures to match unwanted dollar changes in assets or liabilities with offsetting dollar changes in a futures position. A fully hedged position is where a change Δ in cash market position C is offset with an equal but opposite change in the futures position F. For example, a $1 million price decline in a bond portfolio (cash market position) is offset by a $1 million price increase in the value of the futures market position. The result is no loss or gain. The risk of price change has been eliminated.

$$\Delta \text{ Cash price} \qquad = \Delta \text{ Future price} \qquad\qquad (5\text{--}2)$$
$$\Delta \text{ C} \qquad\qquad\quad = \Delta \text{ F}$$

Because changes in the price of the cash commodity and the price of futures contracts are not the same, it is necessary to determine the number of futures contracts required to compensate for the difference in price sensitivity. The sensitivity, measured by a *hedge ratio* (HR), is determined by dividing the percentage change in the cash instrument by the percentage change in the futures instrument.

$$HR = \frac{\%\Delta C}{\%\Delta F} \qquad\qquad\qquad\qquad (5\text{--}3)$$

Suppose that a 12 percent change in the cash price is associated with a 6 percent change in the futures price. The hedge ratio is 2 (12%/6% = 2). A hedge ratio of 2 means that the cash instrument is twice as volatile as the futures contract. To obtain price equivalency, multiply the change in the futures price by the hedge ratio.

$$
\begin{aligned}
\Delta \text{ Cash price} &= \Delta \text{ Futures price} & \times & \quad \text{Hedge ratio} & (5\text{--}4) \\
\Delta \text{ C} &= \Delta \text{ F} & \times & \quad \text{HR} \\
12\% &= 6\% & \times & \quad 2
\end{aligned}
$$

Weighted Hedges

Conversion Factors

To compensate for the greater price sensitivity of the cash position, futures prices may be weighted by the conversion factors, basis point values, or duration. We will examine each of them in order. Other methods of weighting are also used, but are not discussed here.[4]

Weighting a hedge with conversion factors provides the correct number of contracts. That number may be determined by:

$$
\text{No. of futures contracts} = \frac{\text{Par value of cash bonds} \times \text{Conversion factor}}{\text{Par value of futures contracts}}
$$

$$(5\text{--}5)$$

For example, assume that the par value of bonds, which are the cash security, is $1 million. The conversion factor is 1.4296. The par value of U.S. Treasury bond futures contracts is $100,000. Using these figures, 14 futures contracts are required in the hedge. The 14.29 is rounded to 14.

$$
14.296 = \frac{\$1 \text{ million} \times 1.4296}{\$100,000}
$$

Any weighting system has limitations. The principal limitation of using conversion factors is basis risk. Recall that futures prices tracks the CTD security, and that the CTD security is subject to change. If the cash position being hedged is not the CTD security, the futures position will deviate from the cash position.

Basis Point Value

Basis point value (BPV) is the dollar change in the price of a debt security in response to a one basis point (0.01%) change in yield of that security. If the yield on a 9 percent bond with 25 years to maturity increased from 9 percent to 9.01 percent (one basis point), the price of that bond would decline $0.9870 for every $1,000 face value (or $98.70 for $100,000 face value). The dollar value of basis points depends on the coupon rate, maturity, and the level of yields. If the yield on a 25-year zero coupon bond increased from 9 to 9.01 percent, the price of the bond would decline $0.265 for every $1,000 face value. The price of a zero coupon bond with only five years to maturity would decline $0.308 for every $1,000 face value (See Table 5.4).

BPV weights change over time and as yields change. Nevertheless, the advantage of using BPV in a hedge is that it gives price sensitivity to yield changes in absolute dollar terms. The hedge ratio weighted by basis point values is:

$$HR = BPV_{cash\ security} \times \frac{CF}{BPV_{futures\ contract}} \qquad (5\text{-}6)$$

where CF and $BPV_{cash\ security}$ are for the cheapest-to-deliver security.

By way of illustration, consider a bond portfolio with a face value of $500,000. The portfolio consists of five bonds, each having a BPV of $90 per $100,000 face value. The total BPV for the entire portfolio is $450 (5 × $90 = $450). The CTD security has a BPV of $70 per $100,000, and a CF of 1.3959. To have a minimum variance hedge, the BPV of the cash and futures positions must be the same. Using equation 5–5, the correct number of contracts is 9.

$$HR = BPV_{cash\ security} \times \frac{CF}{BPV_{futures\ contract}}$$

$$HR = \$450 \times \frac{1.3959}{\$70}$$

$$= 8.97 = 9$$

Table 5.4   **Basis Point Value**
                (Yield changes from 9% to 9.01%)

Bonds		BPV/$1,000	BPV/$100,000
9%	25 yrs.	$0.9870	$98.70
6%	25 yrs.	0.7460	74.60
0%	25 yrs.	0.2650	26.50
0%	5 yrs.	0.308	30.80

Risk Duration

Duration (D) was explained in Chapter 3. It is the weighted average time to receive all cash flows from a financial instrument, such as bonds or mortgage loans. For purposes of hedging, we are concerned with the duration of the interest rate risk to be hedged, rather than the duration of a security. The duration of the risk is the period of time from today until the day when the interest rate risk ends. For example, a bank plans to buy a 25-year bond when it is auctioned in three weeks. The risk duration is three weeks—the time until the bond is acquired. The risk is that interest rates may fall during the three weeks. To hedge against this risk, the bank takes a long futures position (buys) in bond futures. If rates fall, the price of the long bond futures contract will increase.

The following equation is used to calculate the HR:[5]

$$HR = \frac{P(c)}{P(f)} \times \frac{B(c)}{B(f)} \times \frac{D(c)}{D(f)} \tag{5-7}$$

where

P(c)	=	principal of the cash instrument
P(f)	=	principal of the futures instrument
B(c)	=	percent change in the cash instrument
B(f)	=	percent change in the futures instrument
D(c)	=	risk duration of the cash instrument
D(f)	=	maturity of the futures instrument

Consider the following scenario. On July 10, a bank agrees to make a $20 million fixed rate loan for 360 days beginning on September 1. The loan will be funded with 90-day CDs, which will be sold each quarter (Sept., Dec., March, June) at the prevailing interest rate. The bank wants to hedge against higher funding costs when the CDs are rolled over, which would reduce their net interest margin. The duration risk is the 360-day period of the loan. The bank will use three-month Treasury bill futures to hedge the risk. The contract size for T-bill futures is $1 million. It is expected that the CDs will change 1.25 percent for every 1 percent change in the T-bill futures. This relationship is called the yield beta. More will be said about yield betas shortly. Using these facts,

P(c)	=	principal of the cash instrument	$20 mill.
P(f)	=	principal of the futures instrument	$1 mill.
B(c)	=	percent change in the cash instrument	1.25
B(f)	=	percent change in the futures instrument	1.0
D(c)	=	risk duration of the cash instrument	360 days
D(f)	=	maturity of the futures instrument	90 days

and using equation 5-7, a total of 100 contracts are required to hedge the loan. The bank sells short 25 futures contracts each quarter, for a total of 100 over the 360-day period. Long and short hedges are explained next.

$$ HR = \frac{P(c)}{P(f)} \times \frac{B(c)}{B(f)} \times \frac{D(c)}{D(f)} $$

$$ = \frac{\$20 \text{ mill.}}{\$1 \text{ mill.}} \times \frac{1.25}{1} \times \frac{360}{90} $$

$$ = 100 $$

Hedging Strategies

There are a variety of hedging strategies that may be used to reduce interest rate risk. Long and short hedges are the two basic types of hedges explained here. Other hedges explained here are variants of them. The following examples have been simplified for purposes of illustration. A list of selected references is provided at the end of this chapter for those who want to know more about the futures market before committing their funds.

Long Hedge

A long hedge is also called an *anticipatory hedge* because the hedger anticipates buying a cash commodity. It involves the purchase (going long) of futures contracts *now* in anticipation of buying a cash commodity at a *later* date. The long hedge locks in the purchase price of the cash commodity. In the case of financial futures, a long hedge protects against falling interest rates (higher prices) by fixing interest rates on future investments.

When buying a futures contract, the customer does not pay the market price or the face value. Instead, the customer makes a deposit, called *margin*, to assure performance of the contract. For example, the *initial margin* required by the CBOT on a T-bond futures contract with a face value of $100,000 is $2,700 at the time of this writing. Prices of futures contracts change daily, and margin/commodity accounts are *marked to market*. This means that gains and losses in accounts are collected daily. The minimum *maintenance margin* for T-bond futures is $2,000. Accounts falling below that amount will be required to put up additional margin. This is also the amount the CBOT requires for hedging (*hedge margin*). Margin requirements are different for other futures contracts, and they are subject to change. Moreover, brokerage firms may have different margin requirements. The point here is that buying $100,000 T-bond futures contracts only requires the deposit of the initial margin requirement plus commission. Additional margin deposits may be required during the life of the contract.

The following example illustrates a conversion factor weighted long hedge. Next month, a bank plans to buy $2 million in high yielding CTD Treasury bonds. To lock in the high yields now, the bank buys 29 December T-bond futures contracts at $104-00. This hedge is weighted by the conversion factor, which is 1.4465. The number of futures contracts to be used in the hedge was determined by using equation 5-6.

$$\text{No. of futures contracts} = \frac{\text{Par value of cash bonds} \times \text{Conversion factor}}{\text{Par value of futures contracts}}$$

$$= \frac{\$2,000,000 \times 1.4465}{\$100,000} = 28.9 = 29$$

The total value of the futures contracts is $3,016,000 (29 × $104,000 = $3,016,000). Recall that the bank does not pay that amount. It only makes the required margin deposit.

Over the next few weeks interest rates decrease. The bonds that the bank planned to buy at par (100-00) are now selling at 110-00. To buy the bonds at the higher price would cost an additional $200,000. This amount represents an opportunity cost if the purchase had not been hedged. However, by using a long hedge, the bank can sell the T-bond futures contract at a profit. The price of the T-bond futures contracts increased from 104-00 to 111-000, resulting in a gain of $203,000. The bank also realized a $3000 profit on the transaction as shown in Table 5.5.

Short Hedge

A short hedge is the second basic type of hedge to be examined. In the following examples, it is used to lock in the prices of assets or liabilities when interest rates are expected to increase.

A bank currently holds $1 million face value long-term CTD Treasury bonds priced at 106-08 (106 and 8/32nds) with a cash market value of $1,062,500. The forecast is for interest rates to increase sharply. The bank is concerned about the value of the bonds, and wants to lock in the price. To protect against falling prices, the bank uses a CF weighted

Table 5.5   **Hedging an Anticipated Purchase of Treasury Bonds**

Cash Market	Futures Market
Now	
Plans to buy $2 million	Buys 29 December
T-bonds @ 100-00	T-bond contracts @ 104-00
Total: $2,000,000	Total: $3,016,000
Later	
Buys T-bonds @ 110-00	Sells 29 December
Total: $2,200,000	T-bond contracts @ 111-00
	Total: $3,219,000
Net Change	
– $200,000	+ $203,000
Difference	+$3,000

short hedge. The conversion factor is 1.3403; and 13 futures contracts are required for the hedge. Therefore, the bank sells short 13 T-bond futures contracts at 84-00 (See Table 5.6). The bank does not intend to deliver the bonds that it owns to offset the short position in the futures market.

Subsequently, interest rates increase, and the prices of both the bonds and futures decline. The market value of the bonds declined $100,000. Because the bank was short the futures contracts, it covered (bought) the contracts at a lower price than it sold them, and made $117,000 on that transaction. The bank not only offset the $100,000 decline in the value of the bonds, but also made a profit of $17,000.

Cross Hedge

Cross hedging refers to hedging a cash market risk in one commodity (security) with a futures contract in a different, but related commodity (security). For example, domestic CDs can be cross hedged with Eurodollar futures. Eurobonds, corporate bonds, and mortgage-backed securities can be hedged with Treasury futures. Such hedges are based on the premise that the price movements of the two commodities are highly correlated. Even when they are highly correlated, there is basis risk between the cash instrument and the futures contract. The relationship between the cash and futures instruments is called the *yield beta*.

The yield beta is the correlation coefficient obtained by regressing yield changes in the hedged instrument against yield changes in the CTD security.[6] One problem with regressions based on past data is that history may not repeat itself, particularly in the short run. An alternative is to adjust the HR by expectations about future market relationships.

Suppose that a bank holding a Eurobond portfolio, with a $10 million face value, is concerned about interest rates increasing in the next 90 days. The portfolio has a current market value of $9,825,000. There is no exchange-traded futures contract on Eurobonds to short hedge to protect the value of the cash position. Therefore, the bank decides to use five-year Treasury note (CTD) futures to cross-hedge. These futures contracts have the highest yield beta (0.886) of any of the alternatives futures contracts (ten-year T-notes, T-bonds).

The BPV of the $10 million Eurobond portfolio is $3,890.70. The BPV of five-year futures is $36.95 per $100,000. Based on the BPVs, the HR is 105 contracts.

$$HR = \frac{\$3,890.70}{\$36.95} = 105.3 \text{ contracts}$$

Because the bank is cross-hedging, the yield beta 0.886 must be taken into account. A yield beta of less than one means that Eurobonds tend to lag behind Treasury notes in response to changes in market yields. Multiplying the HR by the yield beta compensates for the lag by

---

Table 5.6   **Hedging Treasury Bonds with Futures Contracts**

Cash Market	Futures Market
Now	
Holds $1 mill. face value	Sells 13 June
T-bonds @ 106-08	T-bond contracts @ 84-00
Total: $1,062,500	Total: $1,092,000
Later	
Holds $1 mill. face value	Buys 13 June
T-bonds @ 96-08	T-bond contracts @ 75-00
Total: $962,500	Total: $975,000
Net Change	
– $100,000	+ $117,000
Difference	+$17,000

---

reducing the number of contracts that will be sold. The adjusted HR is 93 contracts.

HR = 105 contracts × 0.886 yield beta = 93 contracts

This example assumes a parallel shift in the yield curve of the cash and futures commodities. Only one adjustment is made for yield beta. Because of the dynamic nature of two markets in a cross hedge, continuous adjustments of the HR and yield beta are necessary.

The bank sells short 93 T-note futures contracts at 105 to hedge the Eurobond portfolio, which has a current value of $9,825,000. Over the next 90 days, interest rates increase. The value of the Eurobond portfolio declines by $196,500. The bank covers the short at 97-29, and realizes a profit of $194,719. The loss to the bank is $1,782, which is substantially less than if it had not hedged (See Table 5.7).

Strip and Stack Hedges

During a period of rising interest rates, a bank wants to lock in the cost of variable rate three-month CDs that will be issued over the next nine months. As shown in Table 5.8, the bank plans to issue $30 million in CDs in November, and $20 million and $10 million in the next two months. The bank hedges this risk with Eurodollar futures contracts. Eurodollar futures contracts have a face value of $1 million, and a BPV

Table 5.7   Hedging Eurobonds with Futures Contracts

Cash Market	Futures Market
Now	
Holds Eurobonds	Sells 93
	5-year T-notes @ 100-00
Total: $9,825,000	Total: $9,300,000
Later	
Holds Eurobonds	Buys 93
	5-year T-notes @ 97-29
Total: $9,628,500	Total: $9,105,281
Net Change	
– $196,500	+ $194,719
Difference	–$ 1,782

Table 5.8   **Example of Strip and Stack Hedging**

Date	CDs to be funded	Eurodollar futures price	Number of Contracts	
			Strip	Stack
Nov.	$30 mill.	95.77	30 Dec.	60 Dec.
Feb.	$20 mill.	95.55	20 Mar.	30 Mar.
April	$10 mill.	95.17	10 June	10 June

of $25. Technically, this is a cross hedge, and the example involves a short hedge, but we are not interested in those aspects of it. We are interested in strip and stack hedges.

A *strip hedge* involves the use of successive contract months in order to match the maturity dates on the contract with repricing dates in the cash position. For example, on October 5, the bank sells short 30 December Eurodollar contracts to cover the exposure from October through the end of November. At the same time, it also shorts 20 March contracts to cover the exposure from October through the end of February, and 10 June contracts to cover the exposure from October through the end of April. A total of 60 contracts are sold, covering the exposure of the CD issues.[7] Each of the contracts will be covered (bought) when they mature.

The approximate number of contracts needed per million dollars for each element of the strip is found by dividing the BPV of the principal being raised for the 91-day period by the BPV of the futures contract.

$$\frac{1,000,000 \times 0.0001 \times \dfrac{91}{360}}{25} = 1.011 \text{ contracts} \qquad (5\text{--}8)$$

The stack hedge is based on the expectation that the contracts can be rolled over at prices (spreads) that are more favorable than with a strip hedge. The *stack hedge* in this example involves shorting 60 contracts for the nearest pricing period. Recall that 60 contracts were required to cover the exposure for the entire period. The entire exposure is "stacked" in the nearby contract (December). At the end of November, 30 contracts are covered. Then the remaining 30 contracts are rolled out of the December contract (covered), and they are sold short into the March contract. At the end of February, 20 contracts are covered. The remaining ten contracts are rolled out of the March contract and into the June contract. They are covered at the end of April (see Table 5.8).

The Eurodollar futures prices shown are those available in October. The current spread between December and March is 22 basis points. The stack bets that the spread will be larger when the time comes to roll over the contracts. The effectiveness of these strategies depends on the volatility of cash rates, the shape of the yield curve, and the basis. The effects of volatility tend to be dampened by the strip, and are accentuated by the stack. Futures prices that reflect a normal shaped yield curve tend to favor a strip hedge strategy.[8]

Changing Effective Maturity/Rate Sensitivity

In a previous example, we used a long hedge to lock in the purchase price of a cash commodity. Another way to think about a long hedge is that it lengthens the effective maturity (increase interest rate sensitivity) of holdings of a cash commodity. For example, suppose that a bank wants to buy $10 million in Treasury bills for six months. The bank can lock in the rate of return to be earned by (1) buying six-month Treasury bills, or (2) simultaneously buying three-month bills and Treasury bill futures. The latter strategy creates a *synthetic* six-month Treasury bill by combining a cash position with a futures position. For example, exactly 91 days before the June delivery date for Treasury bill futures, a bank buys (1) a three-month Treasury bill, and (2) a three-month Treasury bill futures contract calling for the delivery of Treasury bills in September. In September, the bank takes delivery of the three-month bills. The bank has created a synthetic six-month Treasury bill by using a futures contract. In doing so, it extended the effective maturity and interest rate sensitivity of the three-month Treasury bill cash position.

The bank in this example has a net long futures position. That is, there is a greater dollar volume of long contracts than short contracts. A net short position means the opposite. Table 5.9 shows the effects of net futures positions on asset/liability management. The table shows that a net short position shortens the effective maturity and rate sensitivity of assets and increases it for liabilities. A net long position has the opposite effect. This table shows how financial institutions can have greater control over their interest rate risk.

Synthetic Loan

The notion of a "synthetic" instrument was introduced in the previous example. Another way to use interest rate futures contracts is to synthetically convert a floating-rate loan into a fixed-rate loan. A construction

Table 5.9   **Hedging Applications for Asset/Liability Management**

Net Futures Position

	Short	Long
Assets	Decreases rate sensitivity of assets	Increases rate sensitivity of assets
Liability	Increases rate sensitivity of liabilities	Decreases rate sensitivity of liabilities

company, fearing increasing interest rates, wants to borrow $3 million at a fixed rate for 120 days. However, the bank was only willing to lend that amount on a floating-rate basis. The bank wanted to reprice the loan every thirty days at their CD rate plus three percentage points. The initial interest rate on the loan was 12.00 percent.

The problem was resolved by using a short hedge and interest rate futures to "convert" the floating-rate loan into a fixed-rate loan for the borrower, thereby creating a synthetic loan. The details of the hedge are shown in Table 5.10. On September 1, it shorts three 90-day futures contracts on Treasury bills, each with a face value of $1 million. The yield on the contracts was 10.00 percent, and they were priced at 90.00. The price is an index developed by the International Monetary Market (IMM). It is the difference between the actual T-bill yield and 100.00. Therefore, a T-bill yield of 10.00 percent is quoted on the IMM at 90.00 (100.00 − 10.00 = 90.00).

But that is not the actual price of a 90-day T-bill since the yield and the IMM index are based on annualized rates. The actual price of a $1 million face value T-bill is $975,000.[9] For ease of exposition, the IMM index is used here. The index moves in the same direction as the future purchase price of the deliverable bill. If the index goes up, the price of the underlying bill has increased (interest rates declined). Each basis point (0.01) of the index is worth $25.

Interest on the loan for the September 1 to October 1 period is $30,000 (12.00% × $3 million/12 months = $30,000). This is an important figure to keep in mind because it is the maximum monthly interest cost that the construction company will pay.

On October 1, the construction company covered (bought) one Treasury bill futures contract at the current market price (IMM index) of 90.25. This contract was covered at a $625 loss, because interest rates declined and the price of the contracts increased. However, because interest

Table 5.10   **Synthetic Loan**

	Dates					
	9/1 – 10/1	10/1 –10/30	10/30 –11/30	11/30 –12/30	Totals	Average
Loan $3 million						
Floating interest rate	12.00%	11.75%	11.60%	11.50%	11.71%	Average
Interest cost	$30,000	$29,375	$29,000	$28,750	$117,125	
Futures Contracts						
	Sell 3 (9/1)	Buy 1 (10/1)	Buy 1 (10/30)	Buy 1 (11/30)		
Yield	10.00%	9.75%	9.60%	9.50%		
IMM index	90.00	90.25	90.40	95.00		
Profit (Loss)		($625)	($1,000)	($1,250)	($2,875)	
Net Borrowing Cost						
Effective interest rate	12.00%	12.00%	12.00%	12.00%	12.00%	
Interest	$30,000	$30,000	$30,000	$30,000	$120,000	

rates declined, they only had to pay the bank $29,375. The $625 loss from the futures contract plus the interest payment of $29,375 add to $30,000, the same amount as paid in the previous period.

The construction company repeated the process on October 30. They covered the second contract at a loss of $1,000. This loss occurred because interest rates declined. Nevertheless, their lower interest payment to the bank plus the loss in the futures market came out to $30,000. A similar process was repeated in the next period.

Total losses on futures contracts amounted to $2,875. This amount does not include brokerage fees or the opportunity costs of the funds advanced on margin calls. These amounts were negligible. Total interest cost on the loan, $117,125, plus the $2,875 loss from the futures contracts, amounts to $120,000. It would have been the same cost if they'd had a fixed rate loan for the period.

The effect of using the interest rate futures market was to convert the floating-rate loan into a fixed-rate loan. Although they accomplished this goal, they would have been better off with a floating rate loan because rates declined. Twenty-twenty hindsight is a wonderful thing.

Spread Trading

Spreading refers to the simultaneous purchase of one futures contract and the sale of another, with the expectation that the relationship between their prices will change enough to produce a profit when the positions are closed. An increase in the price differential between the two contracts causes the spread to become positive (widen), while a decrease causes it to become negative (narrow). The crucial factor is the way the contract prices move in relation to one another, rather than the direction of the price change. Spreading can be done between different delivery months (*calendar spread*), or between different but related commodities (*intercommodity spread*), such as bonds and notes, Treasury bills and Eurodollars, the deutsche mark and Japanese yen.

Spreads are widely used because they reduce risk and they lower costs. Because spreaders hold both long and short positions in the same or related commodities, they are usually less risky than an outright long or short position. This is why exchange margins on spreads are lower than those on commodity trades. The margin required for a spread between Treasury notes and Treasury bonds is $500 compared to $2,000 for bonds and $1,000 for notes.[10] Similarly, the margin requirement for a spread between a MidAmerica Commodity Exchange deutche mark and Swiss franc is $425 compared to $650 margin for an outright position in deutsche marks and $750 in Swiss francs.

FOB Spread

An FOB spread is between five-year Treasury note futures and Treasury bond futures. Treasury note and bond futures contracts each have a $100,000 face value. This intercommodity spread takes advantage of the interest rate sensitivity of the two securities involved. As a general rule, the prices of long-term securities (Treasury bonds) and related futures contracts are more sensitive to yield changes than the prices of intermediate-term securities (Treasury notes) and related futures. Therefore, if yields on both intermediate and long-term securities are expected to increase by the same amount (a parallel shift in the yield curve), bond prices would be expected to decline more than note prices (see Figure 5.1). The spread widens. The strategy if the spread widens is to buy the FOB—buy notes futures and sell the bond futures at T, the current time period. Once the spread has widened in the next period T+1, the positions are closed out.

If yields are expected to decline, and the Treasury spread narrows, sell the FOB. That is, sell note futures and buy bond futures in time period T. Once the spread has narrowed in time period T+1, close out the positions. Thus, the general rule is buy the FOB when the spread widens and sell the FOB when the spread narrows.

The following numerical example illustrates buying the FOB spread. In October a banker believes that interest rates are going to increase. She decides to buy one five-year Treasury note futures contract and sell one Treasury bond futures contract. This is called a 1:1 ratio spread because an equal number of contracts were bought and sold. The initial FOB spread—the difference between the two futures prices—was 43/32nds. In November, there was a parallel shift in the yield curve, which increased 23 basis points. The spread widened to 75/32nds, and the positions were closed out. The total gain on the spread was $1,000 (see Table 5.11).

Nonparallel Changes in Yield Curves

Nonparallel changes in yields, and changes in the shape of the yield curve, provide opportunities for weighted (ratio) spreading strategies. Yields change at different rates when the yield curve is flattening or

---

Figure 5.1   FOB Spread

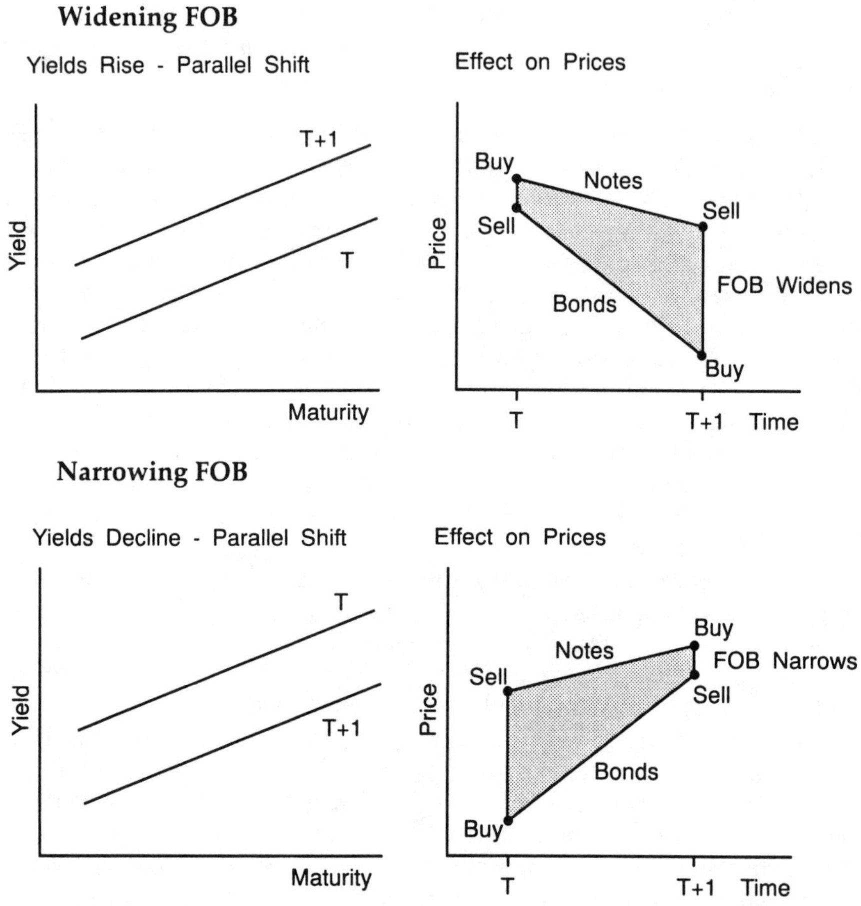

Widening FOB

Narrowing FOB

---

steepening. For example, in a steepening yield curve environment with declining yields, increases in intermediate-term prices may outpace increases in longer-term prices. In such cases, spreads may be bought or sold on a weighted (ratio) basis. The following example illustrates a basis point value (BPV) ratio spread. The scenario is that yields are expected to decline; but yields on ten-year notes are expected to decline faster than yields on long term Treasury bonds. The strategy is to buy the NOB (ten-year T-note futures and T-bond futures) spread, which means buy note futures and sell bond futures. However, the spread is

Table 5.11   **Illustration of FOB Spread**

Inputs	5-year T-note futures	T-bond futures	FOB spread (in 32nds)
October 10			
Yield	7.90%	8.15%	
Dec. futures price	100-14	99-03	43
November 18			
Yield	8.13%	8.38%	
Dec. futures price	99-17	97-06	75
Gain (loss)	(0-29)	1-29	32

Summary
    0-29 loss on 1 long 5-year note contract   ($906.25)
    1-29 gain on 1 short T-bond contract $1,906.25
    Total gain $1,000.00

weighted to equate the BPV of the ten-year T-note to the BPV of the T-bond to keep the price sensitivity of the two instruments constant. The equivalency ratio of note contracts per bond contract may be determined as follows:

$$\text{Equivalency Ratio (Notes per Bond)} = \frac{\text{BPV}_{\text{CTD Bond}}}{\text{BPV}_{\text{CTD Ten-year Note}}} \times \frac{\text{CF}_{\text{CTD Ten-year Note}}}{\text{CF}_{\text{CTD Bond}}}$$

(5–9)

where
    CTD = cheapest to deliver
    CF   = conversion factors

Using equation 5-9, the equivalency ratio for this spread is 1.20 notes per bond. This means buy 1.20 notes for each bond sold. In this spread, 12 note futures contracts are purchased and 10 bond futures are sold.

$$\frac{\$91.12}{\$60.80} \times \frac{1.1501}{1.4358} = 1.20 \text{ notes per bond}$$

During the period shown, yields on 10-year notes declined 50 basis points while yield on T-notes declined 41 basis points. The price gains on the notes were offset by the greater price gains on the bonds; thereby keeping the NOB spread unchanged. Consequently, had this been an unweighted spread (1:1 ratio), there would be no gain or loss. By weighting the spread, the gain is $5,562.50 (see Table 5.12).

Conclusion

In this chapter, it was shown how to use interest rate futures hedges to reduce risk and to increase income of particular cash positions (*micro hedges*). The same thing can be done for large portfolios of assets and liabilities (*macro hedges*). However, hedging is not without costs and risks. While hedging effectively reduces interest rate risk, it also limits opportunities for profit performance. Because market conditions change constantly, dynamic hedging or constant adjustments in the hedged positions are required to achieve desired results. Even then there are basis risks, margin calls, and regulatory considerations. Thus, users must weigh the costs against the benefits.

Selected References

Burghardt, Galen, Morton Lane, and John Papa. *The Treasury Bond Basis: An In-Depth Analysis for Hedgers, Speculators, and Arbitrageurs.* Chicago: Probus Publishing Co., 1989.

CBOT Financial Instruments Guide. Chicago Board of Trade, 1987.

Commodity Trading Manual. Chicago Board of Trade, 1989.

Table 5.12	**Illustration of NOB Spread**		
	10-year T-note Futures	*T-bond Futures*	*NOB Spread (in 32nds)*
June 10			
Yield CTD	10.38%	10.63%	
June futures price	86-06	80-06	+192
June 20			
Yield CTD	9.88%	10.22%	
June futures price	88-31	82-31	+192
Gain (loss)	2-25	(2-25)	unchanged
	× 12 (long)	× 10 (short)	
Totals	$33,375.00	($27,8 12.50)	+$5,562.50

Interest Rate Futures for Institutional Investors. Chicago Board of Trade, 1987.

Fabozzi, Frank J., and T. Dessa Fabozzi, *Bond Markets, Analysis, and Strategies.* Englewood Cliffs, N.J.: Prentice Hall, 1989.

Fabozzi, Frank J., and Irving M. Pollack, eds. *Handbook of Fixed Income Securities.* 2nd. ed. Homewood, IL: Dow Jones-Irwin, 1986.

Kolb, Robert W. *Understanding Futures Markets.* Glenview, IL: Scott Foresman, 1985.

Peck, A. E., ed. *Selected Writings on Futures Markets: Explorations in Financial Futures Markets.* Book V. Chicago: Chicago Board of Trade, 1985.

Rothstein, Nancy H., and James M. Little, eds. *The Handbook of Financial Futures.* New York: McGraw-Hill Book Company, 1984.

Stoll, Hans R., and Robert E. Whaley. *Futures and Options: Theory and Applications.* Cincinnati, OH: Southwestern Publishing Co., 1992.

Treasury Futures for Institutional Investors. Chicago Board of Trade, 1990.

The Delivery Process in Brief: Treasury Bond and Treasury Note Futures. Chicago Board of Trade, 1989.

Both the Chicago Board of Trade and the Chicago Mercantile Exchange hold seminars and have literature dealing with the topics covered here. Their addresses are:

Chicago Board of Trade
LaSalle at Jackson
Chicago, IL 60604
Phone 1-800-THE-CBOT

The Chicago Mercantile Exchange
30 South Wacker Drive
Chicago, IL 60606
Phone 312-930-1000

Endnotes

1. The total invoice amount = Contract price × Futures settlement price × Conversion factor + Accrued interest.

2. For details see *Treasury Futures for Institutional Investors* (Chicago Board of Trade, 1990); *The Delivery Process in Brief: Treasury Bond*

and Treasury Note Futures (Chicago Board of Trade, 1989); *CBOT Financial Instruments Guide* (Chicago Board of Trade, 1987).

3. For further discussion of the role of the futures market, see Anatoli Kuprianov, "Short-Term Interest Rate Futures," *The CME Financial Strategy Paper*, Chicago Mercantile Exchange (1987).

4. For a discussion of other methods of weighting, see *Interest Rate Futures for Institutional Investors* (Chicago Board of Trade, 1987).

5. This version of the a duration HR came from William A. DeRonne, "Five Steps to Interest Rate Futures Hedging," appears in *Selected Writings on Futures Markets: Explorations in Financial Futures Markets*, Book V, A. E. Peck, ed., Chicago: Chicago Board of Trade, 1985. Also see Ira G. Kawaller, "How and Why to Hedge a Short-Term Portfolio," *The CME Financial Strategy Paper*, Chicago Mercantile Exchange, 1987.

6. *Treasury Futures for Institutional Investors* (CBOT, 1990) 33. The example of cross-hedging is based on this source, 43-44.

7. For additional details, see Mark S. Rzepcznski, "Hedging Interest Rate Risk in the Savings and Loan Industry," *Market Perspectives*, Chicago Mercantile Exchange (November 1988).

8. James A. Hoeven and R. Kint Glover, "The Relative Effectiveness of Stack (Roll) vs. Strip Hedging Strategies," *Strategy Paper*, Chicago Mercantile Exchange, 1987.

9. The price is calculated as follows. The interest on a 90-day Treasury bill is paid at maturity, which is four times per year. Therefore, an annual rate of 10.00 percent is equal to 10.00/4 = 0.02500 for 90 days, or $25,000 per $1 million. The price of the T-bill is the face amount less the interest, or $1,000,000 − $25,000 = $975,000.

10. Margin requirements are subject to change. This requirement is for a 1:1 (unweighted) ratio spread.

CHAPTER 6

INTEREST RATE SWAPS

In this chapter interest rate swaps are introduced, with an emphasis on how they can be used in ALM. Specifically, after introducing the basics of swaps, we consider two simple illustrations of how swaps can be used to hedge interest rate risk exposure.

Next we turn to assessing credit risk. Credit risk presents a larger problem for swaps than for futures and forwards. Therefore, we examine in detail the important factors to consider when evaluating exposure to credit risk. Finally, we examine some of the recent variations on the standard interest rate swap. In Appendix 6 the pricing of the standard interest rate swap is explained in detail.

Swap Basics

Interest rate swaps were born out of a need to manage the increased interest rate volatility after the Federal Reserve Board's 1979 decision to allow interest rates to move freely. Today swaps are actively traded on different currencies, interest rates, and energy prices.

An *interest rate swap* is a contract between two counterparties who agree to exchange an interest payment based on a *notional principal* tied to a floating rate, in exchange for an interest payment tied to a fixed rate. The notional principal is the amount on which interest payments are calculated, for example, $1 million. At no time does the $1 million actually trade hands. This type of swap is referred to as a *plain vanilla* swap.

Interest rate swaps are used for a variety of reasons, including (1) reducing financing costs, (2) enhancing yields, (3) hedging, (4) speculating, and (5) arbitrage based on financial position, tax position, or regulatory position. Our interest here is on hedging interest rate risk stemming from asset/liability management considerations. It is important to realize that there are other participants in the swap market with different motives that sometimes lead to bargain prices.

Focus Box   **Interest Rate Swap Terminology**

Advanced Settled—Refers to interest rate swaps in which the cash exchanges are made as soon as the floating rate is set.

Counterparties—Parties involved in the swap.

Fixed Rate Payer—The counterparty who pays based on the fixed rate and receives based on the floating rate.

Floating Rate Payer—The counterparty who pays based on the floating rate and receives based on the fixed rate.

Interest Rate Swap—A contract with two counterparties to exchange an interest payment tied to a floating rate for an interest payment tied to a fixed rate based on a notional principal.

Maturity Date—The date when the swap matures, the last day on which interest accrues.

Notional Principal—The amount which determines the actual dollar payment based on the corresponding interest rates.

Reset Date—The date when the floating rate is set.

Reset Frequency—The number of times per year the floating rate is set, typically quarterly or semi-annually.

Settlement in Arrears—Refers to interest rate swaps in which the cash exchanges occur one period after the floating rate is set.

Swap Rate—The fixed rate of interest in the swap, also known as the **coupon** or **strike rate**.

Basic Structure of a Swap

Two parties are involved in an interest rate swap: the financial institution providing the swap and the client who wishes to enter into a swap. Consider a client who desires to pay fixed rates (and receive floating rates), called the *fixed rate payer*. Suppose this client raised $1,000,000 in a floating rate issue which has semi-annual interest payments and is for a maturity of three years. After one year has past, the client is concerned that short-term interest rates will rise sharply and would like to lock in the current fixed rate. The client could enter a two-year, semi-annual interest rate swap to hedge the floating interest rate risk.

Figure 6.1 illustrates the cash exchanges between the bank and the client on a pay fixed swap (from the client's viewpoint). From the bank's viewpoint this is a pay floating swap, which is denoted the *floating rate payer*. The figure shows that the floating rate payment on the issue is being provided by the bank in return for a fixed rate payment. Actually, in a swap only the net cash payments are exchanged.

In this two-year swap there are three remaining *reset dates* (1/2 year, 1 year, and 1 1/2 years). Reset dates are the days on which the floating rate is set. Figure 6.2 illustrates this pay fixed swap from the client's viewpoint. The bank's viewpoint is exactly the opposite.

Swaps are settled in two ways. *Settlement in arrears* means the floating rate payment is made one period after the floating rate is set. *Advanced settle* means the cash payment is made on the reset date when the floating rate is set. Figure 6.2 illustrates settlement in arrears. The floating rate payment exchanged in one-half year is determined today (at 0) and is denoted $R_{fl,0}$; the floating rate payment exchanged in one year is determined in one-half year (denoted $R_{fl,1}$; the counter is the reset date on which the floating rate is set) and so on.

Figure 6.3 illustrates this same swap but with advanced settle. P() stands for the present value. That is, in advance settle contracts the proceeds are received one period early. The actual payment is the present value of the cash payment. Notice in this two-year swap that all cash exchanges are completed in one and one-half years. Advanced settle contracts resolve credit risk one period earlier.

In conclusion, a pay fixed swap is the same as a portfolio of FRAs, which were explained in Chapter 4. This is illustrated in Figure 6.4. Thus, swap rates can be determined in a similar fashion as FRAs. (For more details see Appendix 6.)

Figure 6.1   **Cash Exchanges between Bank and Client**

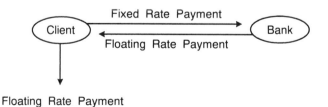

Figure 6.2   **Illustration of Cash Payments of a Two-Year,**
              Semi-Annual, Pay Fixed Interest Rate Swap
              (Settlement in Arrears)

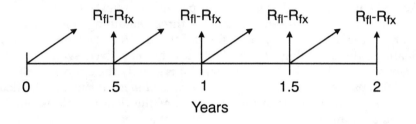

Swaps and ALM

Example (Hedge Floating Rate Liability)

Suppose that a bank holds a two year, $1 million, fixed rate, semi-annual interest only loan which is funded with floating rate deposits. Hence, because rate sensitive assets are less than rate sensitive liabilities (RSA<RSL), the bank is negatively gapped. The market value of the bank's equity is negatively related to floating interest rates. As rates rise, the bank's asset values fall, while the value of the liabilities remains virtually unchanged. Alternatively, as rates rise, the expenses related to

Figure 6.3   **Illustration of Cash Payments of a Two-Year,**
              Semi-Annual, Pay Fixed Interest Rate Swap
              (Advance Settle)

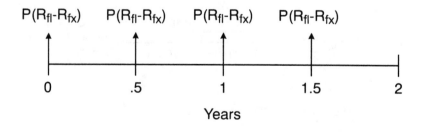

Figure 6.4   **A Pay Fixed Swap as a Portfolio of Forwards**

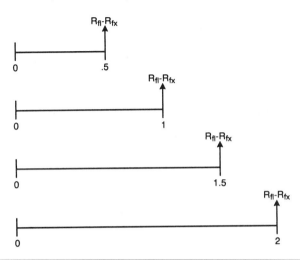

deposits increase but revenues related to the loan remain unchanged, reducing net interest income.

Let's define the situation in more detail. Let $R_{d,fl}$ denote the dollar amount of interest payment of a floating rate deposit liability, and $R_{l,fx}$ denote the dollar amount of the interest payment of a fixed rate loan. Clearly, if rates rise, the value of the assets falls and the value of the equity will decline. With the above definitions, we can express net interest income as $NII = R_{l,fx} - R_{d,fl}$.

Both the interest received on the loan and the interest paid on deposits consist of two components. First, there is the underlying market interest rate. This rate is determined by prevailing market conditions when the loan is made and when the deposits reprice. Also, this rate is a function of the compounding method such as 360- or 365-day year. Second, there is the mark-up by the bank on the loan and mark-down on the deposit. That is, loans are made at a spread above market rates in order for the bank to profit. The same is true for deposits.

We let R_{fx} and R_{fl} represent the fixed and floating rate payments without this mark-up. We let SP denote the spread between the fixed and floating rate payments originally anticipated (which could be lost in a rate move). That is, net interest income can be expressed in two ways.

Net Interest Income $= R_{1,fl} - R_{d,fx} = R_{fl} - R_{fx} + Sp$

For example, suppose the yield curve was flat and the loan initially was made at LIBOR + 1%, and the deposits were offered at LIBOR −1%. Therefore, $R_{fl} - R_{fx}$, which will be based on LIBOR, is 2%. (1% on the loan and −1 on the cost of deposits.)

By way of illustration, suppose LIBOR was initially at 7 percent flat and was not expected to change. Then:

$R_{fl} = R_{fx} = \$1,000,000\ (1/2)\ 0.07 = \$35,000$

$Sp = \$1,000,000\ (1/2)\ 0.02 = \$10,000$

Thus, the anticipated net income before operating expenses is $10,000 ($35,000 − $35,000 + $10,000) on a semi-annual basis.

Figure 6.5 (Panel A) illustrates the unhedged bank's earnings (UBE) over the next two years where R_{fl} is based on expectations. If R_{fl} increases, then our spread will decline.

Figure 6.5 (Panel B) illustrates the cash exchanges on a pay fixed swap (with settlement in arrears) which is unrelated to the bank. The cash exchanges of the swap to the bank do not necessarily have to be positive (as illustrated). That is, if floating rates fall, then the pay fixed swap will require payment rather than receipt. That is, when ($R_{fl} - R_{fx}$) is negative, the bank must pay this difference to the pay floating counterparty.

Figure 6.5 (Panel C) illustrates the results of this bank's hedging strategy. We see the bank has completely neutralized its exposure to interest rate risk. Therefore, with swaps we were able to transform the positively gapped bank into a bank with no gap. Swaps are a very powerful tool in gap management.

There are four major implications which can be drawn from this simple example. First, the swap completely eliminated the risk of higher interest rates. Second, the swap completely eliminated the possibility of increasing earnings if interest rates fall. These two implications are captured in Figure 6.6. Figure 6.6 illustrates the opportunity gains and losses from employing swaps when rates change. If rates rise, we will benefit from swaps. However, if rates fall, we would have preferred not using swaps. Thus, swaps are a two-edged sword. Risk is neutralized but so is return. That is, realized returns with the swap are entirely independent of interest rate changes.

Third, if there is significant quantity risk, a swap could inflict severe damage. For example, suppose the fixed-rate loan was prepaid

Figure 6.5   A Positively Gapped Bank's Earnings with a Swap

Panel A: The Unhedged Bank's Earnings

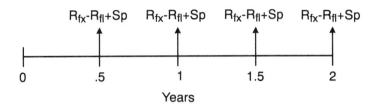

Panel B: A Pay Fixed Swap

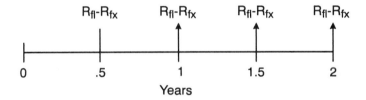

Panel C: A Hedged Bank's Earnings

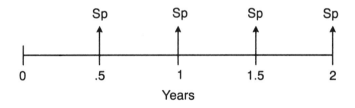

when rates were low and the bank was unable to replace it. In this situation the bank is paying on the swap but is not receiving on the underlying. Finally, credit risk is introduced. That is, the risk that the counterparty fails to perform must be considered. Credit risk will be examined in detail after the next example.

Figure 6.6   **Opportunity Gains and Losses of a Negatively Gapped Bank Hedging with Swaps**

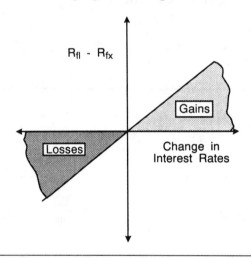

Example (Hedge Floating Rate Asset)

Suppose a bank owns a two-year, $1 million, floating rate, semi-annual loan that was purchased with fixed rate deposits. In this case, the bank is positively gapped and the value of the equity is positively related to floating interest rates. Let $R_{1,fl}$ denote the dollar amount of interest payment of the floating rate loan related to the assets, and $R_{d,\ fx}$ denote the dollar amount of the coupon payment of a fixed rate deposit related to the liabilities.

As before, we let Sp denote the spread between the floating and fixed rate payments originally anticipated (which could be lost in a rate move). Figure 6.7 (Panel A) illustrates the bank's anticipated earnings over the next two years. Clearly, we see if R_{fl} declines, our spread will be lost.

Figure 6.7 (Panel B) illustrates the cash exchanges on a pay floating swap (with settlement in arrears). The cash exchanges to the bank do not necessarily have to be positive. That is, if floating rates rise, then the pay floating swap will require payment rather than receipt. Specifically, when $(R_{fx} - R_{fl})$ is negative, the bank must pay this difference to the pay fixed counterparty.

Figure 6.7   A Negatively Gapped Bank's Earnings with a Swap

Panel A: **The Unhedged Bank's Earnings**

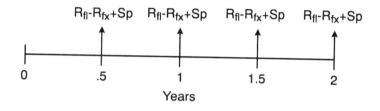

Panel B: **A Pay Floating Swap**

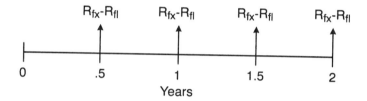

Panel C: **A Hedged Bank's Earnings**

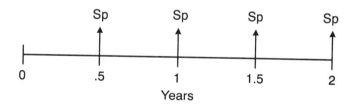

Figure 6.7 (Panel C) illustrates the results of this bank's hedging strategy. We see the bank has completely neutralized its exposure to interest rate risk. Therefore, with swaps we were able to transform the negatively gapped bank into a bank with no gap.

The implications of this simple example are the same as those for the previous one. The exceptions are that the risks are from lower interest rates. Figure 6.8 illustrates the opportunity gains and losses from using swaps when rates change. Thus, this bank's earnings are entirely independent of interest rates.

Credit Risk

Credit risk on a swap is the risk that the counterparty fails to perform as the counterparty is contractually bound. The loss exposure is the cost of replacing the swap when it has positive value. Clearly, if the counterparty defaults when the swap has negative value, there is no loss to your institution. Credit risk is greatest when the counterparty is adversely affected at the same time when the swap moves against the counterparty, for example, a negatively gapped institution which also has a large number of pay floating swaps. For when rates rise, then the value of the institution falls and the value of the swaps also falls.

Credit risk cannot be hedged like interest rate risk. That is, two offsetting swaps increase the credit risk exposure as opposed to eliminating it.

Figure 6.8   **Opportunity Gains and Losses of a Negatively Gapped Bank Hedging with Swaps**

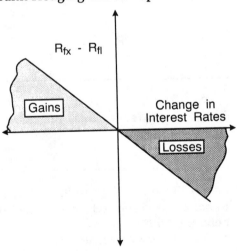

Credit risk exposure over the life of a swap can in general be depicted as illustrated in Figure 6.9. Because most swaps have zero initial
cost, there is zero initial credit risk. However, if right after the swap is
entered rates move dramatically, then the swap will have a large market value and, therefore, a large credit exposure. However, swap performance occurs over time, so the credit risk declines.

There are several other factors influencing credit risk, including the
following:

Overall level of rates—There is some empirical evidence that rates
are more volatile when they are high. Thus, higher rates result in
higher volatility (usually), which results in greater default exposure.

Posted performance collateral—If valuable collateral is posted, then
the risk of default is minimal since when default occurs possession
of the collateral is taken.

Reset frequency—(annual, quarterly, monthly) The more frequent
the swap is reset, the sooner you learn of a defaulting counterparty
and defensive action can be taken.

Shape of yield curve—For example, a steep upward sloping yield
curve would imply that the pay fixed side of a swap would first

Figure 6.9   **Illustration of Credit Risk Exposure in a Swap**

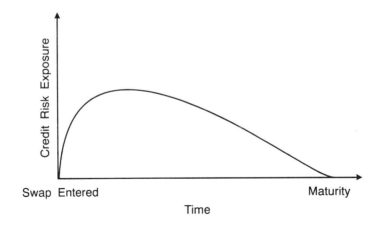

receive payment and later have to make payments. Thus, the credit risk of the pay floating swap is higher because the risk exposure is greater in the future.

Time to maturity of swap—Longer maturity swaps have a longer time period during which default could occur.

Volatility of interest rates—The greater the volatility the more likely the counterparty will face large payments which may trigger default.

Swap Variations

Due to the unique needs of hedgers, several variations of swaps have appeared. Below is a brief listing of different types of swaps:

Amortizing—The notional principal is amortized over the swap. Many loans are amortized, resulting in demand for swap notional principal also to be amortized.

Basis—The swap is between two floating interest rates. The need for a basis swap arises when your assets and liabilities are both floating, but the floating rate is pegged to different interest rates, such as Treasury bills and Eurodollars.

Deferred (forward)—The swap does not begin until a later date. This type of swap is appropriate for a bank with no gap problem in the short maturity range but increasing disparity for longer maturities.

Circus—The swap involves currencies as well as interest rates. This type of swap is useful when managing both currency risk and interest rate risk simultaneously. This swap is most appropriate for multinational banks.

Extendable—One counterparty has the right to lengthen the swap. This feature adds flexibility to the swap holder, allowing the holder to extend the life of the swap if necessary.

Puttable—One counterparty has the right to shorten the swap. This feature also gives the swap holder additional options, specifically, the option to get out of the swap at a specified amount.

Step-up—The notional principal is increased over the swap. This unusual variation is applicable to banks with an increasing gap problem for longer maturities.

Swaption—An option to enter a swap. This is one of the more popular extensions to swaps. A swaption is really an option based product which gives you the right to enter a swap at specified terms.

In recent years there has been a fundamental shift in decision-making related to swaps. In the past, available securities limited the potential strategies for the hedger. Today and in the future, potential strategies determine available products.

Summary

In this chapter, swaps were examined in the context of ALM. We found that swaps are very effective tools for managing interest rate risk. Unfortunately, swaps also mitigate potential gains when rates move in an advantageous fashion.

Credit risk in swaps is a significant consideration, and this risk was examined in detail. Finally, extension to the basic swap design was reviewed.

Appendix 6

Pricing LIBOR-Based Interest Rate Swaps

A swap can be valued in at least three ways: a portfolio of FRAs, a portfolio of a long fixed bond and a short floating bond, or as a collar with the same strike rate (see Chapter 9). Below is the equilibrium swap rate (the fixed rate in the swap) equation based on the FRA approach. We adopt the following notation:

r_s = swap rate
$r_{f,i}$ = forward rate at time i
t_i = time, in days, between reset date i and the payment date
NP_i = notional principal outstanding at time i

The equilibrium swap rate is:

$$
r_s = \frac{\displaystyle\sum_{i=1}^{n-1} \frac{r_{f,i}\left[\dfrac{t_i}{360}\right] NP_i}{\displaystyle\prod_{j=1}^{i}\left[1 + \dfrac{r_{f,j}\, t_j}{360}\right]\left[1 + \dfrac{r_{f,i}\, t_i}{360}\right]}}{\displaystyle\sum_{i=1}^{n-1} \frac{\left[\dfrac{t_i}{360}\right] NP_i}{\displaystyle\prod_{j=1}^{i}\left[1 + \dfrac{r_{f,j}\, t_j}{360}\right]\left[1 + \dfrac{r_{f,i}\, t_i}{360}\right]}}
$$

This derivation is based on the assumption that the swap has an initial value of zero and is based on a 360-day year. Therefore, the present value of the fixed rate payments must equal the present value of the anticipated floating rate payments. We also assume that the best estimate of future floating rates is the forward rate observed today. This assumption is based on the expectations theory of the term structure.

CHAPTER 7

AN INTRODUCTION TO OPTIONS

Option-based asset/liability management concepts are introduced in this chapter. Specifically, we examine the history of option pricing and basic terminology. Also, payoff diagrams for options are illustrated. Finally, hedging interest rate risk is addressed through simple examples. The appendix at the end of the chapter provides the technical details of interest rate option pricing.

The History of Options

Understanding the history of options is helpful in grasping the mechanics and risks of options trading as well as understanding cultural attitudes towards them. An *option* is a legal contract that gives the holder the right to buy or sell a specified amount of the underlying item at a fixed or predetermined price upon exercise of the option. A *call option* gives the right to buy a specified amount of an underlying item. A *put option* gives the right to sell a specified amount of the underlying item. Although puts and calls are traded on the same underlying item, they are separate and distinct securities.

Put and call options are traded on a vast array of underlying items, including stocks, stock indices, interest rates, Treasury bills, Treasury notes, Treasury bonds, Eurodollar CDs, foreign currencies, futures contracts, and commodities.

The earliest record of option trading is usually attributed to ancient Greece around 550 B.C. and the philosopher, mathematician, and astronomer, Thales.[1] The story is recorded in two ways.[2] In one account, Thales foresaw a good olive harvest and so he purchased options (or at least something similar) on the use of olive presses. When the good harvest came, he exercised the options and subsequently leased the presses to the farmers at a considerable profit. The second account states that Thales foresaw a scarcity of olives and subsequently cornered the market by buying contracts giving him the right to buy olives at a pre-determined price.

Copleston states that these accounts of Thales are probably un-true.[3] The telling of stories like these, however, gives support to asser-tions that such activities occurred during Thales's life. Let's move on in history from antiquity to the Roman Empire.

Starting with Julius Caesar (46 B.C.), the Phoenicians and Romans traded contracts with terms very similar to those of current option con-tracts. The most widely cited examples relate to specific contracts on goods that were transported on ship. However, the information related to this period is very sketchy.

In the Middle Ages, we have the Dutch tulip bulb craze. The price of tulip bulbs was rising. During the tulip bulb craze of the first half of the 17th century, an active secondary market developed for call options on tulip bulbs purchased by bulb dealers and put options bought by suppliers. Tulip bulb prices subsequently crashed. It took decades for the Dutch economy to recover from the damage it received from the bursting of the tulip bulb "speculative bubble."

Another example is the South Sea Company in England. In the early 1700s the South Sea Company's stock price experienced explosive growth. An options market developed, and fighting broke out to have the opportunity to purchase shares. When the South Sea Company's stock sank, options were so ill-favored that they were declared illegal for over 100 years.

Option contracts (privileges as they were called) began to appear in the United States in the 1790s, shortly after the Buttonwood Tree Agreement, which established the New York Stock Exchange (NYSE). In the late 19th century, Russell Sage, the "grandfather of modern options trading," organized a system of trading puts and calls on an over-the-counter market and introduced the idea of put-call parity (discussed later).

Interestingly, Louis Bachalier defended his Ph.D. dissertation "The Theory of Speculation" on March 29, 1900, at the Academy of Paris. In his dissertation he single-handedly developed an option pricing model similar to the heat transfer partial differential equation still used today (even before Einstein's work on the heat transfer equation), and pro-ceeded to attempt empirical testing. Unfortunately his dissertation chairman Poincaré) did not like his work primarily because speculation was an unpalatable topic. Thus, it did not receive much attention until the early 1950s when Bachalier's work was rediscovered by Paul Samuelson through L. J. Savage.[4]

In 1901, Arthur Crump argued that trading with options was most prudent.[5] Herbert Filer defended the options market before Congress after the 1929 crash and compared put options to insurance. Because of Filer's defense, in part, the Investment Act of 1934 allows for the existence of option trading, but option trading was regulated by the S.E.C.

The Put and Call Brokers and Dealers Association was created in the 1930s to bring option buyers and sellers together. This market never had widespread appeal because of several limitations, including contracts which:

1. Were nonstandard
2. Were nontransferable
3. Required physical delivery
4. Required no collateral
5. Lacked market makers

Addressing the five concerns listed above, the Chicago Board of Trade (CBOT) created the Chicago Board Options Exchange (CBOE), which began trading 16 call options on stocks on April 26, 1973 at 10:00 A.M. EST.

Coincidentally, Fischer Black and Myron Scholes published a paper on option pricing that has now become a widely used model known as the Black-Scholes Option Pricing Model (BSOPM). Therefore, 1973 was the turning point in option trading history, when options emerged from obscurity into the full light of public trading.

Since 1973, the growth of options markets has been explosive. Table 7.1 provides a chronology of option trading.

We conclude from our study of options that they are tools that may be used for hedging or for speculation. In the latter role, they have been blamed for macroeconomic disruptions, such as the depression following the tulip bulb craze. Now we turn to the basics of trading options.

Basic Concepts

We begin this analysis by examining the basic features of stock options, which afford a modicum of simplicity. Our main interest, however, is interest rate based contracts. Therefore, once the basics are covered, we will move to Eurodollar futures options, which are the most popular contracts today.

Table 7.1   **Modern History of Option Trading**

Year   Activity

1973 —Chicago Board Options Exchange (CBOE) starts trading 16
        call options.

—Black and Scholes publish seminal option pricing paper.

1975 —American Stock Exchange (AMEX) and Philadelphia Stock
        Exchange (PHLX) start trading options.

1976 —Pacific Stock Exchange starts trading options.

1977 —Put options start trading.

—CBOE seeks approval to trade non-stock options.

1979 —U.S. Labor Department declares options use as not being a
        breach of fiduciary duty.

—Comptroller of Currency eases restrictions on bank trust
        departments' use of options.

1980 —Volume of option trading exceeds New York Stock
        Exchange (NYSE) stock volume.

1982 —Kansas City Board of Trade starts trading the Value Line
        Composite Average.

—Chicago Merchantile Exchange (CME) starts trading
        S & P 500.

—New York Futures Exchange starts trading the NYSE
        Composite index.

—CBOE starts trading options on U.S. Treasury bonds.

—PHLX starts trading options on foreign exchange rates.

1983 —CBOE starts trading CBOE 100 stock index options.

1984 —International Money Market at the CME starts trading
        options on futures on foreign exchange.

1985 —CME starts trading Eurodollar futures options.

1989 —Osaka Stock Exchange starts trading the Nikkei 225 options.

An *option buyer* has the right but not the obligation to exercise the
option contract (we say that the buyer takes a *long* position in the option). (See the Focus Box on page 154 for definitions of terms.) If you
bought a call option on a stock, by *exercising* the option contract, you
would receive the stock at the stated price, called the *strike price* or the

exercise price. Likewise, if you bought a put option on a stock, by exercising the option contract, you would sell stock at the strike price.

Suppose that Bill Ups, an eternal optimist, believes that the price of IBM is about to rise sharply soon. Suppose IBM is currently trading for $100. What can he do? He has two choices. First, he can buy 100 shares of IBM stock for a cost of $10,000. This will expose him to considerable loss if prices fall. Second, he can buy call options, which limits his loss if the price of IBM falls, but allows him to profit if he is correct. Hence, call options provide an efficient way to take large positions in securities without exposure to large losses. His loss is limited to the premium paid for the option.

Now suppose that Jane Downs, an eternal pessimist, believes the price of IBM is about to decline. Selling IBM short would expose her to large potential losses. Rather than sell IBM short, she could buy a put option. This limits her losses to the premium if the price increases. She profits if the price declines.

Therefore, option markets provide an efficient way to take advantage of specific opinions regarding the direction of prices at a relatively low cost. Another benefit of the option market is that it allows investors a way to mitigate losses while still participating in gains by buying put or call options.

Recall that a call option on IBM with a strike price of say $105 gives Bill Ups (the call buyer) the right to buy IBM at $105 (denoted IBM 105). An IBM 105 put gives Jane Downs (the put buyer) the right (not obligation) to sell IBM (take a short position) at $105.

Now in order for Bill and Jane to purchase these options, there must be people willing to sell the options (option writers). The *option writer* is the person who sells the contract to the buyer for a price, called the *premium*. The option writer receives the option premium when the contract is entered. For someone to buy an option contract, someone must supply or write the option contract. The option writer is obligated to honor the terms of the option contract if the buyer decides to exercise the option. That is, the writer will receive (in the case of puts) or deliver (in the case of calls) the underlying asset at the strike price if the option is exercised. However, there is no obligation to perform if the option expires worthless. Moreover, an option writer may or may not have to perform according to the option contract.

For example, the call writer of IBM 105 calls must deliver to the call buyer 100 shares of IBM at $105. If the market price of IBM is greater than $105, the buyer may exercise the option and the seller must deliver IBM stock. However, if the price of IBM is less than $105, there is no incentive to exercise the option. Clearly, there is no incentive for the call buyer to exercise the option to buy IBM at $105 if IBM is trading for less than $105.

The option writer is also called the *seller* (said to be *short*). However, the option writer is distinctly different from someone who takes a short position in the stocks. The seller may or may not be long the underlying stock.

Focus Box   **Option Terminology**

Option—A contract giving the holder the right, but not the obligation, to buy or sell some item at a stated price before a stated time.

Premium—The amount the option buyer pays for the option, which is the current market price of the option at the time of purchase.

Long—The holder of the option, the option buyer.

Short or **writer**—The person selling to the option buyer, the option seller.

Call Option—An option giving the holder the right to buy an item (such as a common stock) at a stated price before a stated time.

Put Option—An option giving the holder the right to sell an item (such as a common stock) at a stated price before a stated time.

Exercise price or **strike price**—The stated price in the option contract. The buying price for calls and the selling price for puts.

Maturity date—The date on which the option contract matures. An option holder after this date has no rights under the contract.

Exercise—The act of the holder to render the option contract to purchase (sell) the underlying item at the strike price for calls (puts).

European-style—An option which the holder can only exercise on the maturity date.

American-style—An option which allows the holder to exercise on or before the maturity date.

Position—Owning option contracts, either long or short and either put or call.

Moneyness

Moneyness refers to the difference (whether positive or negative) between the price of the underlying asset and the strike price. Let S represent the current market price of the underlying item (for example, the price of IBM stock) and X represent the option exercise price. An *in-the-money* option is one where exercising the option now would generate a profit (ignoring the purchase price). That is, for calls an option is in-the-money if the underlying item is greater than the strike price (S>X). (See Table 7.2.) If the option is American-style you could exercise the call option, pay $X for the stock, and then sell the stock for $S, generating a profit of $S – $X (>0). For example, if IBM is trading for $110 and the strike price is $100, the potential profit is $110 – $100 = $10. For puts, an in-the-money option is where X>S. An *out-of-the-money* option is the opposite of an in-the-money option. Hence, for calls X>S and for puts S>X, implying no incentive to exercise. At-the-money options are where S = X.

The cost of purchasing an option is called the *option premium*. Specifically, the option premium is the price that the option buyer pays to the writer of the option for the rights obtained within the option contract. This premium is *not* a good faith deposit or down payment: it is a nonrefundable cost paid to obtain the option.

A *position* is said to be taken in options when one has purchased or sold a call or put. There are two types of option transactions related to a position: (1) the *opening transaction*, which is any purchase or sale where a new position is established, (2) the *closing transaction*, which is any purchase or sale where an already established position is offset. Any trade will necessarily be either an opening or a closing transaction.

For example, suppose you purchased one IBM June call to open on February 2nd for a premium of $200. Now suppose two months pass

Table 7.2   **Illustration of Moneyness of Options**

| | **American-Style Options** | |
	Call Options	*Put Options*
Market Price >*Exercise Price*	Profit In-the-Money	Loss Out-of-the-Money
Market Price <*Exercise Price*	Loss Out-of-the-Money	Profit In-the-Money

and you sell that IBM June call on April 2nd for $500. This sell transaction would be to close. Hence, after April 2nd you have no option position and you have $300 profit (before transaction costs). After the sale there would be no outstanding position. In other words, a sale of an identical previous purchase is *offsetting*.

With this brief introduction, we are ready to examine options on interest rates. Most interest rate based options are on futures contracts, which were covered in Chapters 5 and 6. The reason for basing interest rate options on futures contracts is that it is easier to deal with a futures contract than an interest rate. For example, consider a call option on LIBOR. What happens if you wish to exercise such an option? Who will make you a LIBOR based loan? Is the lender creditworthy? These considerations have lead the interest rate options market to be based on interest rate futures contracts.

Eurodollar Futures

We use Eurodollar futures options to illustrate some of the fundamental concepts on ALM with options. Before we examine the details of option-based ALM, a few words about Eurodollars and Eurodollar futures are in order. Eurodollars are United States dollars on deposit outside the United States. The interbank market for immediate and forward delivery of these dollars is large and very liquid. For the most part, Eurodollars are dollar balances on the books of London branches of U.S. banks and other major world-class banks. However, the Eurodollar market includes other currencies, such a yen or pounds, deposited in a different foreign nation (and is thus sometimes referred to as the Eurocurrency market).

Eurodollar time deposits at foreign banks are money market securities that are not transferable, and they are available for any short-term maturity. Eurodollar time deposits are more risky than U.S. Treasury securities because they are not guaranteed by any government. Settlement of these deposits usually takes two business days. Also, domestic regulations, such as Federal Reserve Regulation D (reserve requirements), do not apply to them.

Add-on Interest

Eurodollar time deposits are quoted on an add-on yield basis. Add-on interest rates are quoted on the basis of a 360-day year. The add-on interest rate is determined by the following equation:

$$a = \left[\frac{360}{t} \right] \left[\frac{PAR}{D} - 1 \right]$$
                                                                              (7-1)

where the add-on rate is denoted by a, the amount of the deposit by D, the days to maturity by t, and the amount of the loan plus interest to be repaid by PAR.[6]

The Eurodollar futures contract was introduced by the Chicago Merchantile Exchange (CME) in late 1981, and the Eurodollar futures option contract was introduced by the CME in 1984. The futures contract on Eurodollar time deposits is based on a 90-day, $1 million Eurodollar time deposit, but the contract is settled on a cash basis. That is, physical delivery of the contract does not take place. The delivery months are March, June, September, and December. The contracts expire on the second London business day before the third Wednesday of the delivery month which, thus far, has always been Monday. The minimum price movement is one basis point, or $25 per contract (90/360)*(0.0001)*(1,000,000).

Maturities

Eurodollar futures are available for maturities up to four and one-half years. However, the market is very thin for longer maturities. The Eurodollar futures price is quoted at 100 minus LIBOR. For example, from Table 7.3 we see the June futures contract settled at 95.60, which implies a yield of 4.40. Thus, long positions profit when the quoted futures price rise, implying a decline in LIBOR.

Eurodollar Futures Options

Table 7.3 presents Eurodollar futures and futures options settle prices. *Settle prices* are an average of the trading prices of the last few minutes of the day. Settle prices are not the last price of the day, to avoid manipulation.[7] The yield settle is 100 minus the futures settle price. Eurodollar futures options are quoted in percents, where each percentage point is worth $2,500 (each basis point is worth $25). Hence, the June 9600 call is worth $200 (0.08*2,500).[8]

Strike prices are $0.50 for prices below $88.00 and $0.25 for prices above $88.00. There is no daily price limit, and the contract maturity months are the same as the futures contracts.

Table 7.3   **Eurodollar Futures and Futures Option Prices**

Part A: *Eurodollar Futures Prices (in points of 100% of $1 million par)*

	Settle	Yield Settle
March	95.82	4.18
June	95.60	4.40
September	95.21	4.79
December	94.50	5.50

Part B: *Eurodollar Futures Options (in points of 100% of $1 million par)*

Strike Price	Calls – Settle			Puts – Settle		
	March	June	September	March	June	September
9525	0.58	0.44	0.30	0.01	0.10	0.34
9550	0.34	0.28	0.19	0.02	0.18	0.47
9575	0.13	0.15	0.11	0.06	0.30	0.64
9600	0.03	0.08	0.06	0.21	0.48	0.84

Maturities

The Eurodollar futures options are available with maturities for two years, are American-style, and in-the-money options are automatically exercised on the expiration day. The *expiration date* (or *maturity date*) is the date on which the option expires or ceases to exist if the option contract is not exercised. The expiration date is the second London business day before the third Wednesday of the contract month (the same day as futures contracts).

When a new contract maturity is listed for trading, there will be five put and call strike prices: the nearest strike to being at-the-money and plus and minus two strikes. For example, if the nearest strike is 95.00, then the available strikes will be 94.50, 94.75, 95.00, 95.25, and 95.50. A new strike price will be listed for both puts and calls when the underlying futures price closes within one-half a strike price interval of either the second highest or lowest strike. No new strikes will be added if there are less than 20 calendar days until expiration.

Option Trading

Remember, the option buyer has the right but not the obligation to exercise the option contract. If you bought a call option on Eurodollar futures, by exercising the option contract you would receive the underlying asset (a long position in a Eurodollar futures contract) at the exercise price. Because futures profits and losses are accounted for daily, any profit on the futures would immediately be received, and the futures could be sold. Likewise if you bought a put option on Eurodollar futures, by exercising the option contract you would have a short position in Eurodollar futures (EDF) at the strike price.

Let's turn again to our optimist and pessimist. Now Bill Ups, the eternal optimist, believes the June EDF price will rise sharply soon (interest rates will fall). The June futures contract is currently trading at 94.50 for a yield of 5.50 percent (see Table 7.3). What can he do? He can buy the EDF, which requires him to post margin of less than $1,000 per contract. However, this exposes him to considerable loss if prices fall. Alternatively, he can buy call options, which limit his loss if prices fall, but result in a profit if he is correct. A call option on June EDF with a strike price of 96.00 gives Bill Ups (the call buyer) the right to buy EDF at 96.00 (denoted EDF 9600). Hence, call options provide an efficient way to take large positions in securities without exposure to large losses.

Jane Downs, the eternal pessimist, believes EDF prices will fall soon. Selling EDF would expose her to large potential losses. Rather than sell futures, she could buy a put option, which limits losses to the put price, and she will profit if prices fall. An EDF 9525 put gives Jane Downs (the put buyer) the right (not obligation) to sell EDF (take a short position) at 95.25.

Option Prices

Option prices can be decomposed into intrinsic value and time value. The *intrinsic value* (IV) of an option is zero, or the dollar amount that the underlying asset is in-the-money, whichever is greater. That is, the intrinsic value for calls (IV_c):

$$IV_c = \text{Maximum of 0 or } S - X$$

which can be represented mathematically as:[9]

$$IV_c = \max(0, S - X) \tag{7-2}$$

or for puts (p):

$$IV_p = \max(0, X - S) \tag{7-3}$$

The *time value* (TV) of an option is whatever value an option has above its intrinsic value. That is, let C and P represent the call and put prices, respectively, then:

$$TV_C = C - IV_C \qquad\qquad (7\text{--}4)$$

and for puts (p):

$$TV_p = P - IV_p \qquad\qquad (7\text{--}5)$$

From the definitions of time value and intrinsic value, we can represent option prices as:

$$C = IV_C + TV_C = \max(0, S - X) + TV_C \qquad\qquad (7\text{--}6)$$

and:

$$P = IV_p + TV_p = \max(0, X - S) + TV_p \qquad\qquad (7\text{--}7)$$

For example, suppose the current price of an EDF June futures is 95.60 (S = \$95.60). (See Table 7.3.) The current price of an EDF June 9600 put is 48 basis points (P = 0.48, X = 96.00), the put's intrinsic value is 40 basis points (IV_c = \$1,000 (0.40 * \$25)) and the time value is 8 basis points (TV_c = \$1,200 – \$1,000 = \$200 (0.08 * \$2,500)). The EDF June 9600 call is trading at \$200 (0.08 * \$2,500), then the call's intrinsic value is \$0 (IV_p = max (0, 95.60 – 96.00) = 0) and the time value is \$200 (TV_p = \$200 – \$0 = \$200).

Payoff Diagrams

A *payoff diagram* is a graphical means to illustrate either (1) the value of a security (option, stock, futures, and so forth), or (2) the dollar profit or loss, or both (1) and (2) as it relates to the value of the underlying asset at maturity. For example, consider a call option on EDF June contracts with strike price of 9600 (X = 96.00) and call price (or premium) of \$200 (C = \$200).

Figure 7.1a illustrates the price of the call option at maturity (the option's intrinsic value) identified as the Price Line. If the futures price falls below 96.00 at maturity, then the option will expire worthless. If the futures price at maturity is 95.00, the call price is \$0. However, if the futures price rises above 95.00 at maturity, the option is in-the-money and has a positive price. Specifically, for every basis point the futures price is above 96.00, then the option is worth an additional \$25. For example, if the futures price rises to 97.00 (100 basis point increase) at maturity, then the call option will have a price of $2,500 ((97.00 – 96.00)*$2,500).

The price of an option is equal to its intrinsic value (IV_c) plus its time value (TV_c). However, the price of an option at maturity will be equal to just its intrinsic value (because there is no time left, there is no time value). The price at maturity (the Price Line) can be represented graphically as a line emanating from the strike price (96.00 here). If the option expires worthless (out-of-the-money, S<X), then the option holder faces total loss of the premium, which is represented in the figure to the left of 96.00. Next, we examine the dollar profit and loss at maturity.

If the option expires in-the-money, it has intrinsic value. The option investment is said to just *break even* if the proceeds from the exercise of the option at maturity are just equal to the original option premium. Specifically:

$$IV_{c,t} = \max [S - X, 0] = C$$

where t represents the maturity date. For example, when S = 96.08, then $IV_{c,t}$ = C = 8 basis points (bps) and we just break even. Eight basis points equals $200, the cost of the option.

The dollar profit and loss from holding the option (ignoring the time value of money) is identified at the P/L Line (the profit and loss line) and the shaded areas represent profits or losses. Figure 7.1b illustrates the P/L Line for this $200 call at 96.00. If the futures price falls below 96.00 at maturity, then the option is worthless, and the investor is out of the $200 option price. For every basis point the futures rises above 96.00, the investor makes an additional $25. With a $200 purchase price, the futures must rise to 96.08 in order to just break even. For every additional bp above 96.08, the option provides an additional $25 of profit. If the futures price reaches 97.00 at maturity, then the profit from this option is $2,300 ((97.00 – 96.00 – 0.08) * $2,500).

Figure 7.1c combines both the Price Line and the P/L Line, which we term the payoff diagram. We see that the P/L Line lies below the Price Line by exactly the purchase price of the call option. If we shift the price line down by $200, then we would have the P/L Line.

Figure 7.2 illustrates the payoff diagram for writing a call option on EDF 96.00 with C = $200. The value of this short call position at maturity can be described as a line emanating under the horizontal axis to the right of the strike price. The P/L Line is similar except it is shifted up by the $200 premium. If the futures price falls to 95.00, then

Figures 7.1a   **Price Line for Buying a Call Option
(Strike Price = 96.00, Call Price = $200)**

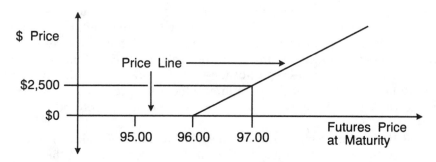

Figure 7.1b   **P/L Line for Buying a Call Option**

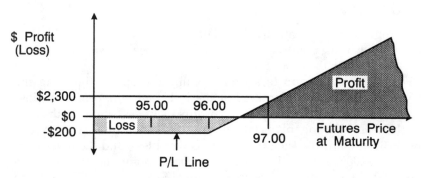

Figure 7.1c   **Payoff Diagram for Buying a Call Option**

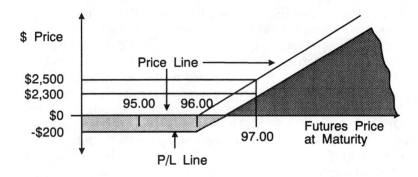

the call writer earns the call premium of $200 and has no obligations at maturity. However, if the futures price rises to 97.00 at maturity, then the writer may lose $2,500 at maturity and have a dollar loss of $2,300 (–2,500 + 200) unless the writer is long the underlying asset, offsets, or hedges potential losses.

Figures 7.1 and 7.2 are just mirror images of each other if the mirror is placed along the futures price axis. For every dollar made in the options market there is a dollar lost. In finance jargon, this is called a "zero-sum game."

In a similar fashion, Figure 7.3 presents the price and P/L lines for buying a put option. Recall that buying a put option in the case of futures gives the buyer the right to sell futures. It will increase in value as the price of the futures declines. The price at maturity is zero if the put option expires out-of-the-money (above 95.25 in our case). The price at maturity is a line rising as the futures price falls below 95.25.

The dollar profit and loss line is merely shifted $250 down from the value at maturity line. For puts the break-even point is:

$$IV_{p,t} = \max [X - S, 0] = P$$

If the futures price rises to 96.25 at maturity, then the put option will be worth $0, and the dollar loss will be $250 (the put price). If the futures price falls to 94.25 at maturity, then the put option will be worth $2,500 ((95.25 – 94.25) * $2,500) and the dollar profit will be $2,250 ($2,500 – $250). Buying a put option is similar to buying a call option, except money is earned when the futures price falls. The put payoff

---

Figure 7.2   **Payoff Diagram for Writing a Call Option
(Strike Price = 96.00, Call Price = $200)**

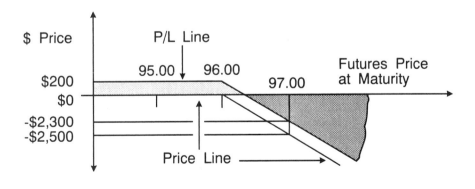

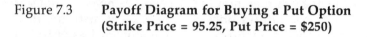

Figure 7.3   **Payoff Diagram for Buying a Put Option**
               (Strike Price = 95.25, Put Price = $250)

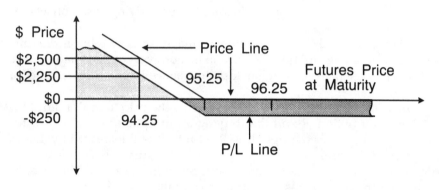

diagram can be viewed as the mirror image of the call, except the mirror is placed vertically on the strike price.

Figure 7.4 presents the Price and P/L lines for writing a put option. Writing puts obligates the option writer to buy a futures from the buyer of the option. When the futures price falls, the option holder will want to exercise the option and sell futures at X. Therefore, the put writer loses as the futures price declines, unless the writer offsets or hedges. The lines in Figure 7.4 are the mirror image of those in Figure 7.3, where the mirror is placed on the horizontal axis.

Interest Rate Options versus EDF Options

Our objective is to manage interest rates. Accordingly, we need to convert futures prices into interest rates. If an option is purchased, one has to pay the premium today. This is represented by the down arrow at "Today" in Figure 7.5 on the time line for both calls and puts. Arrows pointing down represent cash outlays, and those pointing up represent cash receipts.

R_x represents the cash payment made by the seller if the option is exercised, and R_{fl} represents the cash receipt to the seller if it is exercised (only the net proceeds are exchanged). Interest rate options are cash settled, so only the difference of $R_{fl} - R_x$ is paid (for calls). R_x and R_{fl} are determined by interest rate levels, and they represent the dollar interest. In the case of LIBOR:

Figure 7.4 **Payoff Diagram for Writing a Put Option (Strike Price = 95.25, Put Price = $250)**

$ Price
P/L Line
$250
$0
-$2,250
-$2,500
94.25
95.25
96.25
Futures Price at Maturity
Price Line

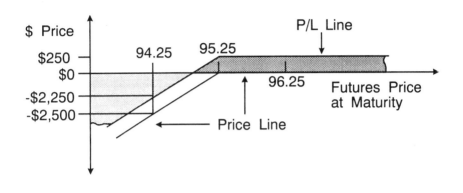

Figure 7.5 **Cash Payments Related to Interest Rate Options**

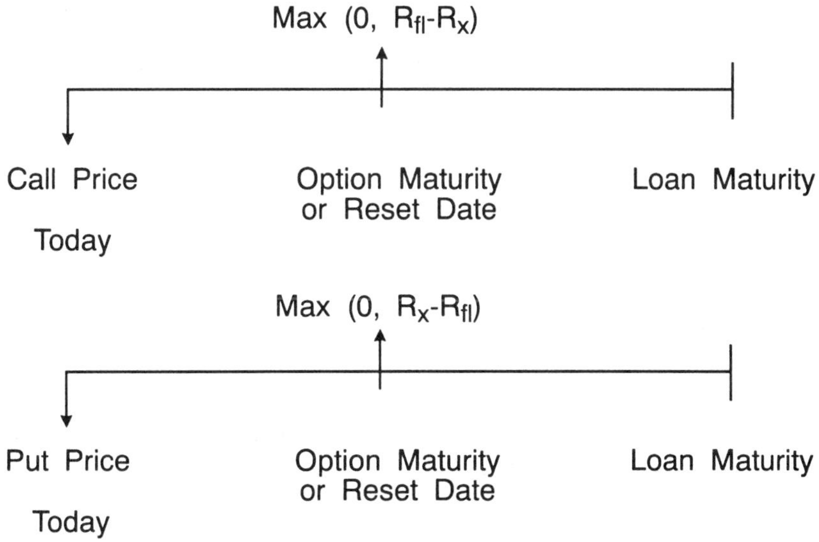

Max (0, R_fl-R_x)
Call Price
Today
Option Maturity or Reset Date
Loan Maturity
Max (0, R_x-R_fl)
Put Price
Today
Option Maturity or Reset Date
Loan Maturity

$$R_x = NP \left[\frac{t}{360} \right] r_x \qquad\qquad (7\text{-}8)$$

$$R_{fl} = NP \left[\frac{t}{360} \right] r_{fl} \qquad\qquad (7\text{-}9)$$

where r_x is the LIBOR interest rate set in the option contract, r_{fl} is the prevailing LIBOR interest rate at a specified date known as the *reset date* (which is also known as the option maturity date), t is the number of days in the loan, and NP is the notional principal. From equations 7–2 and 7–3 we have the intrinsic value of an interest rate call and put:

$$IV_C = \max [0, R_{fl} - R_x] \qquad\qquad (7\text{-}10)$$

$$IV_p = \max [0, R_x - R_{fl}] \qquad\qquad (7\text{-}11)$$

See Figure 7.5.

Example (Falling LIBOR Rates)

In the previous example, Bill Ups was anticipating that LIBOR interest rates would fall (or futures prices would rise because F = 100 – LIBOR). From Table 7.2, he could buy an EDF 9600 June call for $200 (0.08 * $2,500). A 9600 strike implies r_x = 4% or 0.04. Thus, a call option on EDF can be thought of as a put option on interest rates. That is, as rates fall, EDF calls increase in value because 100 – LIBOR rises. However, as rates fall, the price of interest rate puts rises. EDF calls are equivalent to interest rate puts, and EDF puts are equivalent to interest rate calls.

Suppose Bill was right and in June LIBOR was at 3 percent; his payment at maturity would be (NP = $1,000,000 and t = 90):

$$\max [0, R_x - R_{fl}] = \$1,000,000 * \frac{90}{360} * \max [0, r_x - r_{fl}]$$

$$= \$250,000 * \max [0, 0.04 - .03] = \$2,500$$

For every percentage point LIBOR is below 4 percent, Bill gains $2,500. In our example here, he profits $2,300 ($2,500 – $200).

Example (Rising LIBOR Rates)

As before, Jane Downs is forecasting the LIBOR interest rate would rise (or futures prices would fall). She can purchase an EDF 9525 June put for $250 (0.10 * $2,500) (see Table 7.2). A 9525 strike price implies r_x =

4.75% or 0.0475. Remember, an EDF put is an interest rate call. If she is right, and in June LIBOR was at 5.75 percent, her payment at maturity would be:

$$\max [0, R_{fl} - R_x] = \$1,000,000 * \frac{90}{360} * \max [0, r_{fl} - r_x]$$
$$= \$250,000 * \max [0, 0.0575 - 0.0475] = \$2,500$$

Options and ALM

We turn now to using options within the context of ALM. Although the examples given below are simplifications, we are able to emphasize general concepts.

Example (Need to Borrow)

Suppose that two months from now our bank needs to borrow $1,000,000 in Eurodollars for three months. Figure 7.6 illustrates the cash payments.

The bank is concerned that interest rates will rise over the next two months. Recall the bank could use a forward rate agreement (FRA) to fix the borrowing rate to be based on R_{fx} (the fixed rate in an FRA). However, FRAs incur an opportunity loss. (See Figure 7.7.)

We can resolve this situation at a cost, so that we benefit from lower borrowing costs if rates fall, but fix the rate if rates rise. Consider the cash payments of a two-month call option on three-month rates given in Figure 7.8.

Figure 7.6   **Anticipated Borrowings in Two Months for a Duration of Three Months**

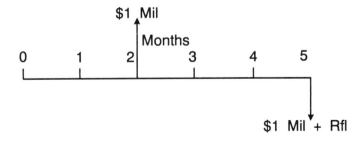

Figure 7.7   **Opportunity Gains and Losses from Using FRAs to Hedge Borrowing Interest Rate Exposure**

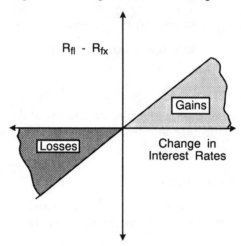

By combining the cash payments shown in Figure 7.6 and 7.8, we have the cash payments given in Figure 7.9.

Assume that the option payment on the option maturity date is deferred to the maturity date of the underlying borrowing10 (see Figure 7.10).

With this simplifying assumption, the net cash payment (NCP) at maturity is:[11]

$$\text{NCP} = -\$1,000,000 - \min [R_{fl}, R_x] \tag{7-12}$$

Figure 7.8   **Cash Payments Related to Two-Month Interest Rate Call Options**

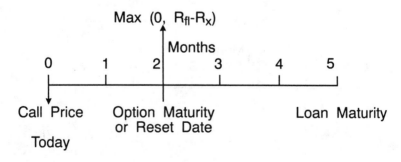

Figure 7.9   **Cash Payments of Both Borrowing and Call Options**

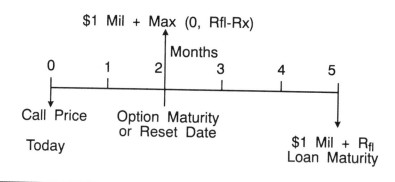

Equation 7–12 illustrates the nice property that our borrowing cost is the lower of the strike payment, R_x, or the floating payment, R_{fl}. However, this benefit was acquired at a cost: the original cost of the option. If we assume that the strike payment is equal to the rate implied in the FRA (that is, $R_x = R_{fx}$), then the opportunity gains and losses can be graphically presented in Figure 7.11.

If rates rise, we will have benefitted from the lower borrowing cost. Also, if rates fall, the loss is limited to the loss of the call price.

From this example of borrowing, we reach the following conclusions:

Figure 7.10   **Cash Payments of Both Borrowing and Call Options, with Settlement in Arrears**

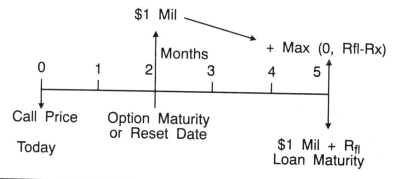

Figure 7.11   **Opportunity Gains and Losses from Using Call Options to Hedge Borrowing Interest Rate Exposure**

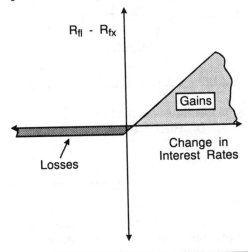

1. The call option sets a minimum on the interest payment at R_x.
2. The opportunity loss is only the price of the call option.
3. The opportunity gains are unlimited as rates rise.
4. If we are unsure as to our borrowing needs, the most we can lose is the option price. Call options are an appropriate tool when there is quantity risk.

Example (Need to Lend)

Suppose that in two months our bank wants to lend $1,000,000 in Eurodollars for a three-month duration. Figure 7.12 illustrates the cash payments.

The bank is concerned that interest rates will fall. The bank could employ an FRA to fix the lending rate to be based on R_{fx} (the fixed rate in an FRA), but that would incur a potential opportunity loss. (See Figure 7.13.)

We can resolve this situation at a cost, so that we can benefit from higher lending rates if rates rise, but fix the rate if rates fall. Consider the cash payments of a two-month call option on three-month rates given in Figure 7.14.

Figure 7.12   **Anticipated Lending in Two Months for a Duration of Three Months**

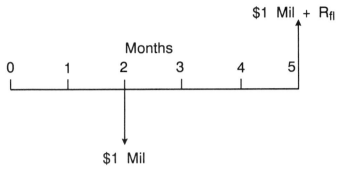

Combining the cash payments exhibited in Figures 7.12 and 7.14, we have the cash payments given in Figure 7.15.

Assume that the option is settled in arrears. That is, we assume the option payments at contract maturity are actually paid at the maturity of the loan (see Figure 7.16).

With this simplifying assumption, the net cash payment (NCF) at maturity is:[12]

Figure 7.13   **Opportunity Gains and Losses from Using FRAs to Hedge Lending Interest Rate Exposure**

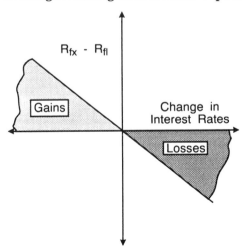

Figure 7.14   **Cash Payment Related to a Two-Month Interest Rate Put Option**

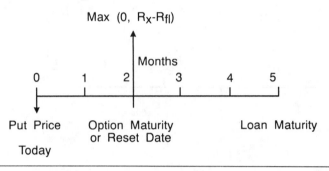

Figure 7.15   **Cash Payments of Both Borrowing and a Put Option**

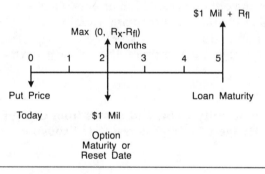

Figure 7.16   **Cash Payments of Both Lending and a Put Option, with Settlement in Arrears**

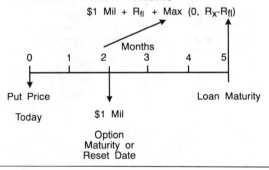

$$NCF = \$1,000,000 + \max [R_{fl}, R_x] \qquad (7\text{–}13)$$

Equation (7–13) illustrates the nice property that our investment return is the greater of the strike payment, R_x, or the floating payment, R_{fl}. However, this benefit was acquired at a cost, the original cost of the put option. Again, if we assume that the strike payment is equal to the rate implied in the FRA (that is, $R_x = R_{fx}$), then the opportunity gains and losses can be graphically presented in Figure 7.17.

If rates fall, we will have benefitted from locking in our investment return. Also, if rates rise, the loss incurred is only the loss of the put price.

From this lending example, we reach the following conclusions:

1. The put option allows us to earn the greater of the strike amount, R_x, or the prevailing amount, R_{fl}.
2. The opportunity loss is only the price of the put option.
3. The opportunity gains are virtually unlimited as rates fall.
4. If we have quantity uncertainty, we can only lose the put premium.

Figure 7.17   **Opportunity Gains and Losses from Using Put Options to Hedge Lending Interest Rate Exposure**

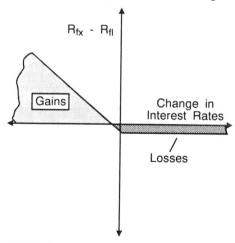

Summary

Options were introduced in this chapter. With a review of history and the basics, we examined Eurodollar futures options in detail. Payoff diagrams were introduced as a means of assessing various trading strategies. A comparison was made of interest rate options and Eurodollar futures options. Interest rate call options are equivalent to Eurodollar futures put options, and interest rate put options are equivalent to Eurodollar futures call options. Finally, we examined the use of options in ALM by way of two simple examples. In the next chapter, we examine the use of caps and floors in ALM.

Endnotes

1. For a detailed history of options see Chapter 1 of Options Institute, eds. *Options: Essential Concepts and Trading Strategies* (Homewood, IL: Business One Irwin, 1990).

2. For more information see Diogenes Laertius, *Lives of the Philosophers*, appears in Fredick Copelston, S.J., *A History of Philosophy (Garden City, NY: Image Books, 1985),* 22-24.

3. See Frederick Copleston, S. J., *A History of Philosophy (Garden City, NY: Image Books, 1985),* 22-24.

4. See P. A. Samuelson, "Rational Theory of Warrant Pricing," *Industrial Management Review,* 6 (Spring 1965) 13-31.

5. See Aurthur Crump, *The Theory of Stock Speculation,* cited in Options Institute, eds. *Options: Essential Concepts and Trading Strategies* (Homewood, IL: Business One Irwin, 1990).

6. See Miles Livingston, *Money and Capital Markets* a Second Edition (Miami, FL: Kolb Publishing Co., 1993).

7. If settle prices were the last trading price, then traders could easily manipulate these prices by entering large orders at the end of the day.

8. The standard quotation convention is to refer to contracts as 9600 rather than 96.00. Thus a June 9600 call is a June call with strike price of 96.00.

9. Note that $IV_c = max$ (a, b) means if a>b, then $IV_c = a$. Max (a, b) means to take the larger of a or b.

10. When we get to caps and floors in Chapter 8, these types of contracts are referred to as *settled in arrears*. That is, the contract payoffs occur one period later.

11. This can be determined by rearranging the NCF in the following way: NCF = $-\$1,000,000 - R_{fl} + \max\{0, R_{fl} - R_x\}$ Moving the $-R_{fl}$ inside the maximum sign and noting that the maximum of two negative numbers is the same as the minimum of two positive numbers, we have the following equivalent expression. For example, if $R_{fl} = \$10,000$ and $R_x = \$7,500$, then: NCF = $-1,000,000 - 10,000 + \max[0, 10,000 - 7,500]$ NCF = $-1,000,000 - 10,000 + \max[-10,000, -7,500]$ = $-1,000,000 - \min[10,000, 7,500]$

12. From Figure 7.16 the net cash payment (NCF) at maturity can be rearranged in the following way to make the interpretation clear.
NCF = $\$1,000,000 + R_{fl} + \max[0, R_x - R_{fl}]$
Moving the $+R_{fl}$ inside the maximum sign, we have equation 7–13.

Appendix 7

Interest Rate Option Pricing

There are numerous technical details in pricing options on interest rates. We present a model below based on a European-style option (no early exercise). The following notation is used:

r_f = Forward LIBOR rate between the option maturity date and the loan maturity date

r_x = Strike rate specified in the options contract

t_s = Number of days until option matures

t = Number of days between the option maturity date and the loan maturity date

To price interest rate options we assume interest rates are lognormally distributed and the best estimate of the future spot rate is today's forward rate. The following interest rate call option pricing equation can be derived:

$$c = A * B * \left[r_f N(d_1) - r_x N(d_2) \right]$$

where:

$$A = \left[\frac{NP * \dfrac{t}{360}}{1 + \dfrac{r_f t}{360}} \right]$$

$$B = \left[\frac{1}{1 + \dfrac{r_s t_s}{360}} \right]$$

$$d_1 = \left[\frac{\ln\left[\dfrac{r_f}{r_x}\right] + \left[\dfrac{\sigma^2}{2}\right]\left[\dfrac{t_s}{365}\right]}{\sigma\sqrt{\dfrac{t_s}{365}}} \right]$$

$$d_2 = d_1 - \sigma\sqrt{\frac{t_s}{365}}$$

and N(d) is the value of a cumulative normal distribution at d.

Similarly, the value of an FRA put option is as follows:

$$P = A * B * \left[r_x N(-d_2) - r_f N(-d_1) \right]$$

Figures 7A.1 and 7A.2 show how sensitive our prices are to changes in underlying parameters. We see that both the strike price and volatility greatly affect the results.

Figure 7A.1   Options and Forward Rates

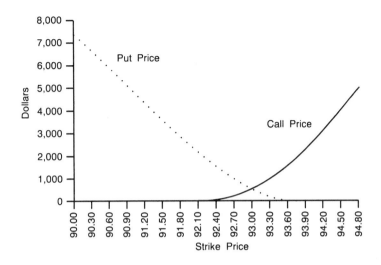

Figure 7A.2   Options and Volatility

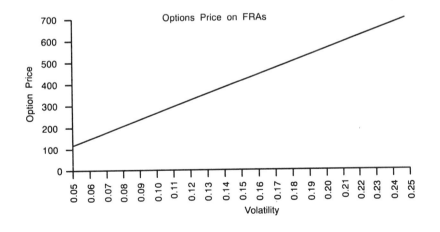

CHAPTER 8

CAPS AND FLOORS

Interest rate caps and floors are introduced in this chapter. After covering the basic terminology and cash exchanges, we turn to using caps and floors in ALM.

After examining credit risk, we close this chapter with some recent variations on standard interest rate caps and floors. In Appendix 8, the pricing of the standard interest rate cap and floor is explained in detail.

Cap and Floor Basics

An interest rate *cap* is a financial arrangement that limits the exposure of a floating rate borrower to upward movements in interest rates. A cap is a series of interest rate call options in which the writer guarantees the buyer whatever additional interest he must pay on his loan if the rate on that loan goes above an agreed rate, R_{XC}.

An interest rate *floor* is a financial arrangement that limits the exposure of a floating rate lender to downward movements in interest rates. A floor is a series of interest rate put options, in which the writer guarantees the buyer whatever additional interest she must pay on her loan if the rate on that loan goes below an agreed rate, R_{XF}. An interest rate *collar* is just the combination of a cap and a floor. Collars are covered in more detail in Chapter 9. Figure 8.1 illustrates the interest cost of loans with caps, floors, and collars. The cap limits the amount paid when rates are high, the floor sets a lower bound on the amount paid when rates are low, and the collar just combines both concepts.

Cash Payments Related to Caps and Floors

The cash exchanges on a long cap can be simplified with the following definition of the future cash exchanges:

$$LC_i = max\left[0, R_{fl,i} - R_{XC} \right]$$

Figure 8.1   **Loan Payments with Caps, Floors, and Collars**

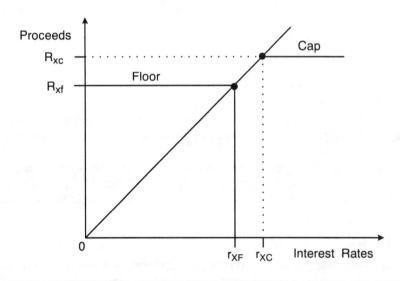

where LC_i is the cash exchanged on a long cap at i, i = 1, ... , n. For example, assume the floating interest rate at the third reset date was 8 percent, the LIBOR-based agreement calls for semi-annual reset dates (say 182 days[1] between the third and fourth reset dates), the notional principal is \$1,000,000, and the strike rate is 7 percent. Then from Chapter 4 we have:

$$R_{fl,3} = \$1,000,000 \left[\frac{182}{360} \right] 0.08 = \$40,444$$

$$R_{XC} = \$1,000,000 \left[\frac{182}{360} \right] 0.07 = \$35,389$$

and

$$LC_4 = \max [0, \$40,444 - \$35,389] = \$5,055$$

The reset dates are always one period before the cash is paid. That is, we assume these contracts are settled in arrears. Figure 8.2 provides an illustration of the cash exchanges.

The cash exchanges on a long floor can be simplified with the following definition of the future cash exchanges:

Figure 8.2   Illustration of Cash Exchanges of a Long Cap

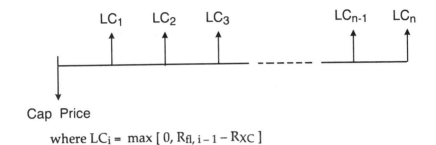

Cap Price

where $LC_i = \max [\, 0, R_{fl,\,i-1} - R_{XC} \,]$

$$LF_i = \max \left[\, 0, R_{XF} - R_{fl,\,i-1} \,\right]$$

where LF_i is the cash flow at i, i = 1, ... , n. Notice that these floors are also settled in arrears. Using the same data as the previous example, but assuming the floating interest rate at the third reset date was 6 percent and the strike rate is 7 percent, we have:

$$R_{fl,3} = \$1,000,000 \left[\frac{182}{360}\right] 0.06 = \$30,333$$

and

$$LF_4 = \max [\, 0, \$35,389 - \$30,333 \,] = \$5,056$$

Figure 8.3 provides an illustration of the cash exchanges.

Figure 8.3   Illustration of Cash Exchanges of a Long Floor

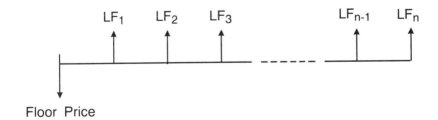

Floor Price

Caps, Floors, and ALM

Let us return once again to the hedging examples given in Chapter 6. We examine these from a different perspective, one of using caps and floors rather than swaps. Which strategy is ultimately preferred is based on preference, but with these examples the issues should be transparent.

Example (Hedge Floating Rate Liability)

A bank owns a two-year, $1 million, fixed rate, semi-annual, interest only loan that was funded with floating rate deposits. Let $R_{d,fl}$ denote the dollar amount of interest payment of a floating rate deposit related to the liabilities, and $R_{l,fx}$ denote the dollar amount of the interest payment of the loan, which is fixed related to the assets.

We let SP denote the spread between the fixed and floating rate payments originally anticipated (which could be lost in a rate move and could be different at different reset dates). Recall that R_{fx} and R_{fl} represent the fixed and floating rate payments without a mark-up (see Swaps and ALM section in Chapter 6). Figure 8.4 (Panel A) illustrates the bank's anticipated unhedged earnings over the next two years. If R_{fl} increases, then the spread will be lost and earnings will decline.

Figure 8.4 (Panel B) illustrates the cash exchanges on a cap (with settlement in arrears). For caps, the cash exchanges to the bank have to be positive or zero. Buying a cap can never result in future negative cash exchanges. That is, if floating rates fall, then the cap will not require any cash exchanges. When $(R_{fl} - R_{XC})$ is negative, the bank is not required to pay the institution that is short the cap.

Figure 8.4 (Panel C) illustrates the results of this bank's hedging strategy.[2] That is, if rates rise, then the cash payment required by the bank's liabilities rises. This adverse move is offset by the cash payment on the cap. However, if rates fall, then the gain accruing to the institution by a widening spread is not offset by the cap (because it is out-of-the-money).

We see the bank has insured its exposure to interest rate risk. Therefore, with caps we were able to transform the negatively gapped bank into a bank with insurance against the interest rate risk. Caps are a very powerful tool in gap management.

There are four major implications of this simple example. First, the caps completely eliminated the risk related to higher interest rates. Second, caps do not eliminate the possibility of increasing earnings if interest

Figure 8.4   A Negatively Gapped Bank's Earnings with a Cap

Panel A: **The Unhedged Bank's Earnings**

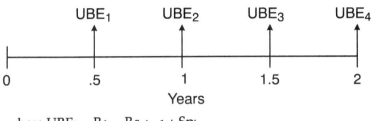

where $UBE_i = R_{fx} - R_{fl, i-1} + Sp_i$

Panel B: **A Two-Year, Semi-Annual Reset Cap**

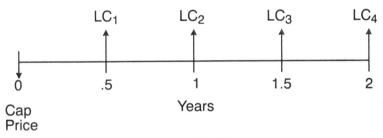

where $LC_i = \max[\, 0, R_{fl, i-1} - R_{XC} \,]$

Panel C: **A Hedged Bank's Earnings**

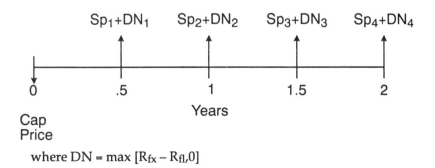

where $DN = \max[R_{fx} - R_{fl}, 0]$

rates fall. These two implications are captured in Figure 8.5 (Panel A). The figure illustrates the opportunity gains and losses from employing caps when rates change. If rates rise, then the bank will be glad that caps were used that offset realized losses to net income. If rates fall, the only loss is the cap price originally paid. Panel B gives the opportunity gains and losses with a pay fixed swap. The differences of these two strategies are transparent. Swaps eliminate both realized gains and losses, whereas caps just eliminate realized losses.

Third, if there is significant quantity risk, caps do not inflict the damage that swaps do. For example, suppose the fixed rate loan was prepaid when rates were low, and the bank was unable to replace it. In this situation the bank might lose the initial cap price paid (less any resale value), but that is all. Finally, credit risk is introduced. That is, the risk that the counterparty fails to perform must be considered. (Credit risk will be examined in detail below.)

Example (Hedge Floating Rate Asset)

Suppose a bank owns a two-year, $1 million, floating rate, semi-annual interest only loan that was purchased with fixed rate deposits. Hence, the bank is positively gapped and the value of the equity is positively related to floating interest rates. Let $R_{l,fl}$ denote the dollar amount of the interest payment of the floating rate loan related to the assets, and $R_{d,fx}$ denote the dollar amount of the interest payment of the deposits.

As before, we let SP denote the spread between the floating and fixed rate payments originally anticipated (which could be lost in a rate move). R_{fl} and R_{fx} are, as defined earlier, payments without a mark-up. Figure 8.6 (Panel A) illustrates the bank's anticipated earnings over the next two years. Clearly, we see if R_{fl} declines, then our spread will be lost.

Figure 8.6 (Panel B) illustrates the cash exchanges on a floor (with settlement in arrears). The cash exchanges to the bank have to be non-negative because the bank buys the floor. That is, if floating rates rise, then the floor will not require any cash exchanges.

Figure 8.6 (Panel C) illustrates the results of this bank's hedging strategy.[3] We see the bank has insured its exposure to interest rate risk. Therefore, with floors we were able to transform the positively gapped bank into a bank that is insured against this exposure.

There are four major implications of this simple example, which are similar to the previous example. First, the floors completely eliminated the risk of higher interest rates. Second, the floor did not eliminate the

Figure 8.5   **Opportunity Gains and Losses of a Negatively Gapped Bank Hedging with Caps or Swaps**

Panel A: **Long Cap**

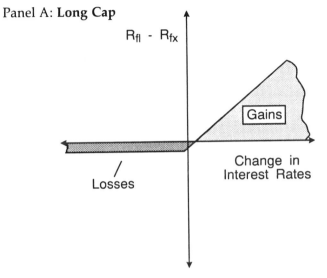

Panel B: **Pay Floating Swap**

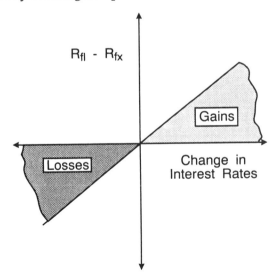

Figure 8.6   A Positively Gapped Bank's Earnings with a Floor

Panel A: The Unhedged Bank's Earnings

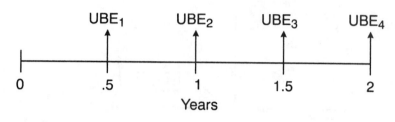

where $UBE_i = R_{fl,\,i-1} - R_{fx} + Sp_i$

Panel B: A Two-Year, Semi-Annual Reset Floor

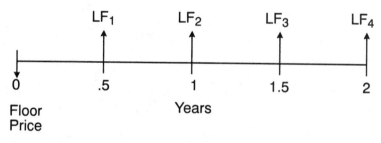

where $LF_i = \max[\,0, R_{XF} - R_{fl,\,i-1}\,]$

Panel C: A Hedged Bank's Earnings

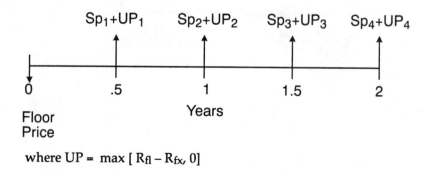

where $UP = \max[\,R_{fl} - R_{fx},\,0\,]$

possibility of increasing earnings if interest rates fall. These two implications are captured in Figure 8.7 (Panel A). The figure illustrates the opportunity gains and losses from employing floors when rates change. If rates fall, then the bank will be glad that floors were employed that offset realized losses to net income. If rates rise, the only loss is the floor price originally paid. Panel B gives the opportunity gains and losses with a pay floating swap. Again, the differences between swaps and floors is transparent. Swaps neutralize the risk, whereas floors insure the risk.

Third, if there is significant quantity risk, then the only loss would be the initial price paid for the floor (less any resale value). For example, suppose the floating rate loan was prepaid when rates were high and the bank was unable to replace it. In this situation the most the bank could lose is the dollar amount of the floor initially paid (less any value that it currently possesses). Finally, credit risk is introduced. That is, the risk that the counterparty fails to perform must be considered. Credit risk will be examined next.

Credit Risk

The credit risk exposure of caps and floors is similar to swaps. Only the long cap or floor faces credit risk. The short will never be due something from the long (and thus cannot default). Credit risk analysis only need be conducted when your institution is long caps or floors (which is typically the case for ALM).

As before, the majority of the credit risk exposure occurs early in the life of the contract. As time passes risk is resolved and credit exposure declines (See Figure 6.9). Early in the life of the contract, large rate moves could result in large potential credit risks. However, as time goes by we have options maturing and the overall value of the contract declining. The only additional factor is the choice of strike rate. Clearly, the more the cap or floor is in-the-money (higher strike rate for floors and lower for caps), the more credit exposure is faced.

Variations on a Theme

There have been several variations to caps and floors. One of the most popular is a swaption. A *swaption* is an option on a swap. Swaptions behave in the same fashion as caps and floors in many respects. *Captions* are options on a cap. That is, you buy an option to buy a cap,

Figure 8.7   **Opportunity Gains and Losses of a Positively Gapped Bank Hedging with Floors or Swaps**

Panel A: **Long Floors**

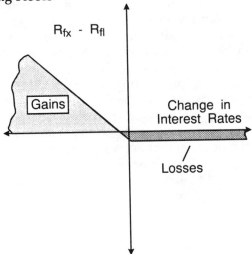

Panel B: **Pay Fixed Swap**

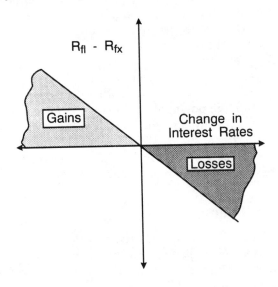

which itself is a portfolio of options on interest rates. Thus, captions are options on a portfolio of options. *Floortions* are options on a floor.

One final variation worth mentioning here is *averaged options*. Averaged options are similar to the standard options in caps and floors, except the floating rate is based on an average rate. These averaged options mitigate the risk that on the reset date the interest rate is atypical.

Summary

In this chapter, the basics of caps and floors are covered. By way of two simple examples the usefulness of caps and floors in ALM was illustrated. Caps and floors are powerful tools in insuring against adverse interest rate moves. We concluded the chapter by addressing credit risk and some recent variations on caps and floors.

Endnotes

1. It should be noted that although LIBOR is quoted on a 360-day year, the interest payments are based on an actual day count.

2. We assume for simplicity that R_{fx}, the fixed rate amount related to the loan, is equal to the cap strike rate amount, R_{XC}. Adding the cash payments in panels A and B, with some rearranging, yields the results presented in panel C.

3. The analysis here is similar to that presented in the previous note.

Appendix 8

Pricing LIBOR-based Caps and Floors

The price of a cap is just the sum of the prices of the embedded call options. That is, the cap price is:

$$CAP = \sum_{i=0}^{n-1} C_i [t_{s,i}]$$

where $C_i(t_{s,i})$ is an interest rate call option that matures at s for the period ending at i.

Similarly, a floor is just the sum of the prices of the embedded put options. That is, the floor price is:

$$FLOOR = \sum_{i=0}^{n-1} P_i [t_{s,i}]$$

where $P_i(t_{s,i})$ is an interest rate put option that matures at s for the period ending at i.

CHAPTER 9

ZERO-COST ASYMMETRIC HEDGES

Interest rate contingent claims that are asymmetric and have zero cost are examined in this chapter. They combine the advantages of swaps with the advantages of caps and floors. The two contracts examined in detail are collars and participation agreements. Both of these contracts are combinations of caps and floors.

The cash exchanges related to these instruments are examined after some basic terminology is explained. Next, the use of these instruments in ALM is covered by way of a simple example. Finally, we assess the credit risk. Appendix 9 discusses pricing collars and participation agreements.

Basics

The basic idea behind the contracts examined here is the desire to receive the benefits of asymmetric hedging without having to pay any up-front fees. The specific benefit is being able to participate in favorable interest rate moves, while at the same time insuring against unfavorable moves. Although this sounds too good to be true, there are contracts that fulfill these demands (but not without costs).

The first contract is an interest rate *collar*. An interest rate collar is a financial arrangement combining caps and floors that limits a floating rate loan payment on both the upward side (cap) and on the downward side (floor). A collar is just short a cap and long a floor (or vice versa).

Suppose that you hold a two-year, semi-annual, LIBOR-based, \$1,000,000, floating rate loan. As in Chapters 6 and 8, let $R_{fl,i-1}$ denote the interest paid on a semi-annual basis. Now if you entered a collar (sell a cap at R_{XC} and buy a floor at R_{XF} [$R_{XC} > R_{XF}$ because we cap high rates and place a floor when rates are low]), then the proceeds at each payment date can be expressed as follows:

$$\text{Proceeds} = R_{fl,\, i-1} - \max[0,\, R_{fl,\, i-1} - R_{XC}] + \max[0,\, R_{XF} - R_{fl,\, i-1}]$$

The proceeds represented above is a combination of the floating rate payment, $R_{fl,i-1}$, paying on the short cap, $\max[0, R_{fl,i-1} - R_{XC}]$, and receiving on the long floor, $\max[0, R_{XF} - R_{fl,i-1}]$. We can express the above equation in a form more transparent:

$$\text{Proceeds} = \begin{cases} R_{XC} & \text{if } R_{fl,i-1} > R_{XC} \\ R_{fl,i-1} & \text{if } R_{XC} > R_{fl,i-1} > R_{XF} \\ R_{XF} & \text{if } R_{XF} > R_{fl,i-1} \end{cases}$$

which is illustrated in Figure 9.1. The line segment labeled 1 in Figure 9.1 represents the proceeds when rates exceed r_{XC}. (Recall from Chapter 4 that lowercase r represents the interest rate, whereas uppercase R represents the payment amount.) Segment 2 represents the floating rate amount when rates are between r_{XC} and r_{XF}. Finally, segment 3 represents the proceeds when rates are below r_{XF}. We see that the proceeds are "collared" between R_{XC} and R_{XF}.

Recall that collars are appealing because they are zero cost instruments. That is, the proceeds from the sale of the cap must exactly offset the cost of the floor. The lower the strike amount on the caps, R_{XC}, the more likely the cap will be in-the-money and, therefore, the higher the

Figure 9.1   **Proceeds to a Floating Rate Lender with a Collar**

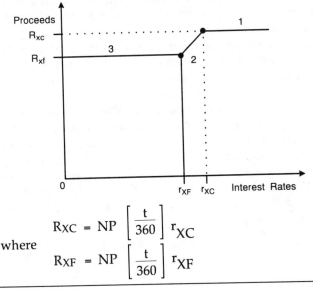

$$\text{where} \quad \begin{aligned} R_{XC} &= NP \left[\frac{t}{360}\right] r_{XC} \\ R_{XF} &= NP \left[\frac{t}{360}\right] r_{XF} \end{aligned}$$

cap premium. However, the lower the strike amount on the floors, R_{XF}, the less likely the floor will be in-the-money and, therefore, the lower the purchase price of the floor. From this we conclude that for a given choice of a floor, R_{XF}, there is one unique cap, R_{XC}, such that the prices are the same and the whole transaction has zero cost. Thus, collars provide a way to purchase interest rate risk insurance if rates fall by selling some of the gains if rates rise.

The borrower could use a similar transaction to hedge the risk of rising interest rates. That is, the borrower could use a collar of the form where the cap is purchased and the floor is sold. In this case, the amount the borrower has to pay is identical to the lender's proceeds.

Participation agreements (PAs) are similar in some respects to collars. PAs involve both caps and floors and are zero cost securities. The difference lies in the strike amount being the same, but the quantity of caps does not equal the quantity of floors.

The basic idea behind a participation agreement is that the construction firm receives a cap on the rate that has to be paid on the floating rate loan. In return, the firm agrees to pay an increasing premium as rates fall. That is, the firm has to participate in its payments as rates fall.

To illustrate PAs, consider a construction loan of $1,000,000 to build a building which will take two years to complete. The bank wants to make a floating rate loan. The firm wants a fixed rate loan because of their concern for rising interest rates. Under a floating rate loan, the firm's net profit is inversely related to interest rates. If rates rise, the firm's earnings will decline, and the probability of default is increased.

Let us illustrate this mathematically. The interest payments from the construction company would be as follows:

$$\text{Payment} = \begin{cases} R_{XC} & \text{if } R_{fl} > R_{XC} \\ R_{fl} + a(R_{XC} - R_{fl}) & \text{if } R_{fl} < R_{XC} \end{cases}$$

where a is some agreed-upon constant between zero and one, $0 < a < 1$. We see from this expression that if rates rise, the firm is protected by having only to pay the cap amount. As rates fall, the firm pays the floating rate plus a premium, which increases as floating rates fall. That is, the firm is paying a greater amount of interest at the very time that it can afford it, when rates are low. As rates fall, the firm participates in paying higher rates (which is beneficial to the bank).

Figure 9.2 illustrates the proceeds to a floating rate lender with a participation agreement. We see that as rates rise, the proceeds are fixed at the cap (segment 1). As rates fall, the borrower pays at an increasing rate (segment 4).

Figure 9.3 illustrates all possibilities covered thus far. A straight floating rate loan is represented by line segments 5, 2, and 6. If we purchase a cap, then the proceeds are represented by segments 5, 2, and 1. (Remember, the cap premium is not represented in Figure 9.3.) Thus, the proceeds have been capped at R_{XC}.

If we only sell a floor, then the proceeds are represented by segments 3, 2, and 6. We set a floor on the proceeds at R_{XF}. (Again the floor premium is not represented.) If we enter into a collar (purchase cap, sell floor), then the proceeds are represented by segments 3, 2, and 1, and there is no premium. We have constrained the proceeds on both sides at R_{XF} and R_{XC}.

If we enter a PA we have capped the proceeds at R_{XC} at the expense of paying proceeds based on segment 4 rather than 2 and 5. PAs do not have an initial premium to be paid. Which strategy is preferable depends on the relative cost (paid initially or forgone opportunity losses) and the user's particular needs and risk preferences. (Issues related to pricing collars and participation agreements are covered in Appendix 9.)

Figure 9.2   **Proceeds to a Floating Rate Lender with a Participation Agreement**

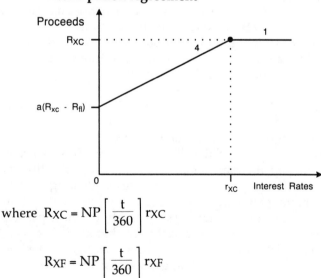

where $R_{XC} = NP \left[\dfrac{t}{360} \right] r_{XC}$

$R_{XF} = NP \left[\dfrac{t}{360} \right] r_{XF}$

Figure 9.3   **Comparison of Proceeds from a Floating Rate Loan with Caps, Floors, Collars, and Participation Agreement**

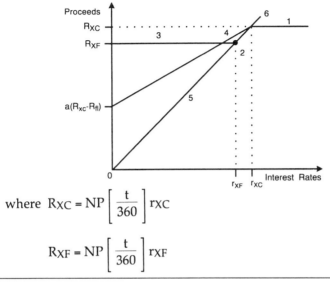

where $R_{XC} = NP \left[\dfrac{t}{360} \right] r_{XC}$

$R_{XF} = NP \left[\dfrac{t}{360} \right] r_{XF}$

We turn our attention now to using collars and participation agreements in ALM.

Collars and ALM

We turn again to the hedging examples given in Chapters 6 and 8. The focus here is on the usefulness of collars on interest rate risk management.

Example (Hedge Floating Rate Liabilities)

Assume that a bank is negatively gapped with fixed rate loans and floating rate deposits. Figure 9.4 (Panel A) represents the unhedged bank's anticipated earnings. If floating rates rise, then deposit-related expenses rise, and earnings will decline. Figure 9.4 (Panel B) illustrates the cash payments on a collar. The collar will have positive cash payments if rates exceed r_{XC}, negative cash payments if rates fall below r_{XF}, and no cash payments if rates remain between r_{XC} and r_{XF}.

Figure 9.4 (Panel C) illustrates the net results of using a collar. The bank receives a benefit when rates rise above r_{XC}, which is a time when

Figure 9.4   **A Negatively Gapped Bank's Earnings with a Collar**

Panel A: **The Unhedged Bank's Earnings**

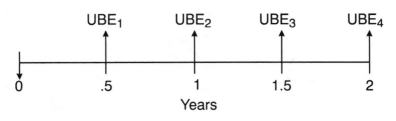

where $UBE_i = R_{fl,\,i-1} + Sp_i$

Panel B: **A Two-Year, Semi-Annual Reset Collar**

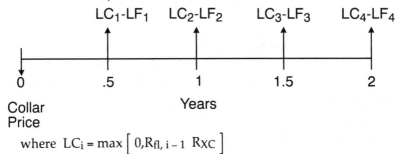

where $LC_i = \max\left[\,0, R_{fl,\,i-1}\ R_{XC}\,\right]$

$$LF_i = \max\left[\,0, R_{XF} - R_{fl,\,i-1}\,\right]$$

Panel C: **A Collared Bank's Earnings**

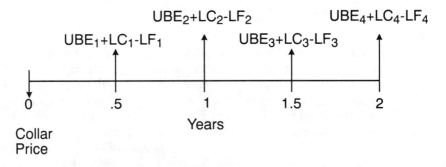

earnings are at risk. The bank pays when rates fall below r_{XF}, which is a time when earnings are the greatest. Thus, the benefits of the cap are not paid today with a cap price, rather they are paid in the future if rates fall (which is a time when the bank can afford to pay).

Figure 9.5 (Panel A) illustrates the opportunity gains and losses when collars are used. If rates rise sharply, we do not suffer losses because we were protected with the cap (and we also receive this benefit "free" if rates remain high). If rates fall, however, we do suffer opportunity losses because potential gains will be lost in the payments required of the collar. From Panel A we see that if $r_{XC} = r_{XF}$, then this is nothing but a pay floating swap. (Move both gain and loss lines to the center and compare with Figure 8.4, Panel B.)

Comparing Figure 9.5, Panel B, with Panel A, we see the relative trade-offs of caps versus collars. Caps afford a larger payoff if rates rise, limit opportunity losses if rates fall, but require an initial investment. Collars provide the same protection if rates rise, face large opportunity losses if rates fall, and do not require any initial investment. Which particular strategy is optimal depends on a number of factors, including the bank's forecast of future interest rates, anticipated volatility, bank capital, and the stability of the bank's gap.

Example (Hedge Floating Rate Assets)

Now assume that a bank is positively gapped with floating rate loans and fixed rate deposits. The analysis of a positively gapped bank with collars is similar. Figure 9.6 illustrates a positively gapped bank's earnings with and without a collar. With a collar the bank is protected against falling rates by paying when rates rise. A positively gapped bank is in a position to pay when rates rise.

Figure 9.7 illustrates the opportunity gains and losses for collars and floors in this situation. Again if $r_{XC} = r_{XF}$, then this is a pay fixed swap (see Figure 8.6, Panel B).

Participation Agreements and ALM

With participation agreements, the insurance provided both to the negatively gapped bank through a cap and the positively gapped bank through a floor is the same as a collar (see Figures 9.8 and 9.9). The difference rests in how this insurance is paid. With collars, the insurance is paid with either a floor or a cap. Participation agreements, on

Figure 9.5   **Opportunity Gains and Losses of a Negatively Gapped Bank Hedging with Collars or Caps**

Panel A: **A Collar (Buy Cap, Sell Floor)**

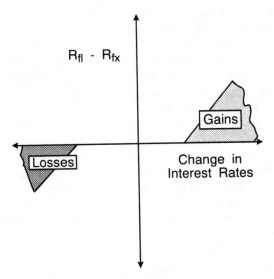

Panel B: **Long Cap**

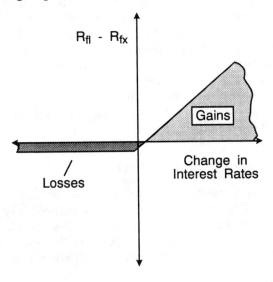

Figure 9.6   A Positively Gapped Bank's Earnings with a Collar

Panel A: The Unhedged Bank's Earnings

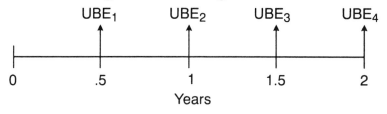

where $UBE_i = R_{fl,\, i-1} - R_{fx} + Sp_i$

Panel B: A Two-Year, Semi-Annual Reset Collar (Sell Cap, Buy Floor)

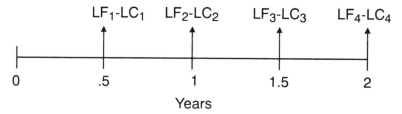

where $LC_i = \max\left[\, 0, R_{fl,\, i-1} - R_{XC} \,\right]$

$LF_i = \max\left[\, 0, R_{XF} - R_{fl,\, i-1} \,\right]$

Panel C: A Hedged Bank's Earnings

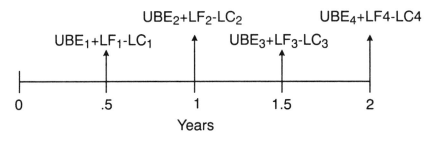

Figure 9.7   **Opportunity Gains and Losses of a Positively Gapped Bank Hedging with Collars or Caps**

Panel A: **A Collar (Buy Cap, Sell Floor)**

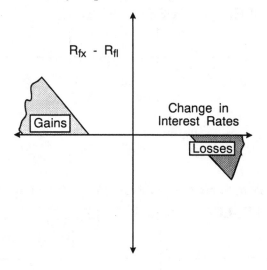

Panel B: **Long Floors**

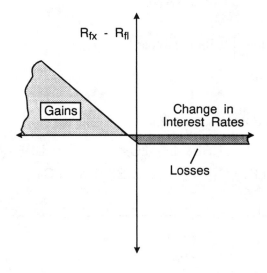

the other hand, pay for the insurance by participation in adverse moves in rates (adverse in the sense of the participation agreement).

The difference between the opportunity gains and losses of collars, and participation agreements for negatively and positively gapped banks are illustrated in Figures 9.10 and 9.11. The trade-offs are clear. For the negatively gapped bank (Figure 9.10), the opportunity losses on a small decline in floating rates is greater for the participation agreement than the collar. The reverse is true for the larger moves. A similar analysis can be made with the positively gapped bank.

Summary

In this chapter, collars and participation agreements are illustrated, with particular focus on ALM. We found that both of these contracts require no initial cash payment. That is, the "cost" of the insurance is paid for by accepting a short position of either a cap or a floor.

These hedging instruments combine the benefits of symmetric hedges (no initial cost) with the benefits of asymmetric hedges (asymmetric payoffs). The optimal choice of which hedging vehicle to use—forward rate agreements, futures, swaps, caps, floors, collars, and/or participation agreements—is very complex. A clear understanding of the costs and benefits of each strategy will no doubt lead to more effective decisions.

Figure 9.8   **A Negatively Gapped Bank's Earnings with a
                Participation Agreement**

Panel A: **The Unhedged Bank's Earnings**

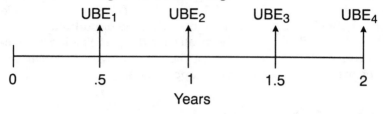

where $UBE_i = R_{fx} - R_{fl,\,i-1} + Sp_i$

Panel B: **A Two-Year, Semi-Annual Reset Participation Agreement
         (With a Cap)**

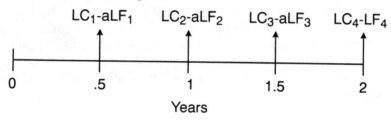

where $LC_i = \max\left[\,0, R_{fl,\,i-1} - R_{XC}\,\right]$

$LF_i = \max\left[\,0, R_{XF} - R_{fl,\,i-1}\,\right]$ $\left(\text{where } R_{XF} = R_{XC}\right)$

Panel C: **A Negatively Gapped Bank's Earnings with Participation
         Agreement**

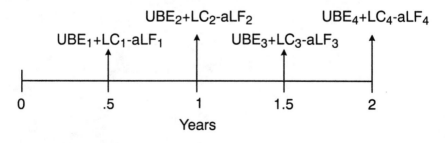

Figure 9.9   **A Positively Gapped Bank's Earnings with a Participation Agreement**

Panel A: The Unhedged Bank's Earnings

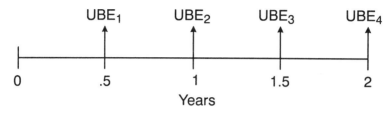

where $UBE_i = R_{fx} - R_{fl, i-1} + Sp_i$

Panel B: A Two-Year, Semi-Annual Reset Participation Agreement (With a Floor)

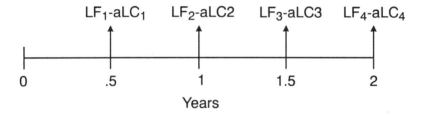

where $LC_i = \max \left[0, R_{fl, i-1} - R_{XC} \right]$

$LF_i = \max \left[0, R_{XF} - R_{fl, i-1} \right] \quad \left(\text{where } R_{XF} = R_{XC} \right)$

Panel C: A Hedged Bank's Earnings

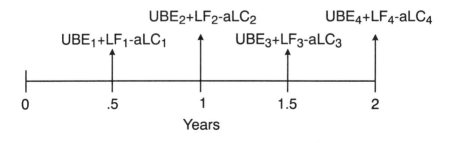

Figure 9.10   **Opportunity Gains and Losses of a Negatively Gapped Bank Hedging with Collars or Caps**

Panel A: **A Participation Agreement (With Cap)**

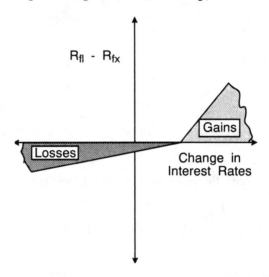

Panel B: **A Collar (Buy Cap, Sell Floor)**

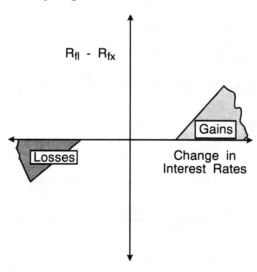

Figure 9.11   **Opportunity Gains and Losses of a Positively Gapped Bank Hedging with Participation Agreements or Collars**

Panel A: **A Participation Agreement (With Floor)**

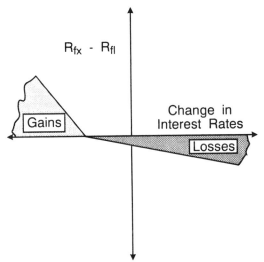

Panel B: **A Collar (Sell Cap, Buy Floor)**

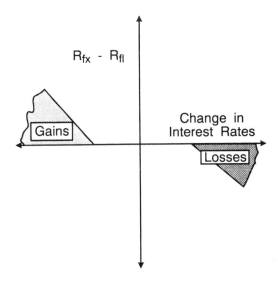

Appendix 9

Pricing Collars and Participation Agreements

The price of a collar is the difference between the prices of a cap and a floor. Recall the price of a cap is the sum of the prices of the embedded call options. That is, the cap price is:

$$CAP = \sum_{i=0}^{n-1} C_i(t_{s,i})$$

where $C_i(t_{s,i})$ is an interest rate call option that matures at s for the period ending at i. Similarly, a floor is the sum of the prices of the embedded put options. That is, the floor price is:

$$FLOOR = \sum_{i=0}^{n-1} P_i(t_{s,i})$$

where $P_i(t_{s,i})$ is an interest rate put option that matures at s for the period ending at i. Thus a collar is:

$$COLLAR = Cap - Floor$$

A participation agreement is very similar, except the strike rates are the same and there is only a proportion of the floor price paid. That is:

PARTICIPATION AGREEMENT = Cap – a * Floor

where a is a constant between zero and 1.

CHAPTER 10

REGULATORY AND ACCOUNTING CONSIDERATIONS

Derivatives Draw Warnings

The headline in *The Wall Street Journal* read "Derivatives Draw Warnings From Regulators."[1] The article stated that some major brokerage firms were expected to take "huge writeoffs" of derivatives. In addition, the derivatives market was temporarily shaken when Drexel Burnham Lambert, Inc., failed, and when the Bank of New England successfully, but with difficulty, unwound its $30 billion portfolio of derivatives and foreign exchange. Moreover, the latest derivatives designed for using advanced computer programs are so complex that neither bank regulators nor the traders' bosses can understand them. The article quoted E. Gerald Corrigan, president of the Federal Reserve Bank of New York, who said that "High tech banking and finance has its place, but its not all that it's cracked up to be . . . I hope this sounds like a warning, because it is."

Corrigan's remarks carry a lot of weight. In addition to Corrigan's position at the Fed, he is also chairman of the Basel Committee on Banking and Supervision of the Bank for International Settlements (BIS). The BIS establishes standards for internationally active banks and securities firms. In this connection, the BIS has established risk-based capital standards for banks. In a joint statement by Richard C. Breeden (Chairman, Technical Committee, International Organization of Securities Commissions) and E. Gerald Corrigan, the BIS announced plans to extend the capital standards to include the interest rate risk of tradeable securities and the price risk in the equity position held by banks.[2] The joint statement reflects the internationalization of global capital markets and the similarity of risks undertaken by both banks and securities firms. It also suggests that more regulations are forthcoming.

Regulations and accounting practices affecting banks using derivatives are extensive and complex, and they are still evolving. Therefore, only general information about them is presented here in order to give readers some understanding of the issues involved. No attempt is made

219

to cover the regulations and practices of every regulatory agency, or the accounting requirements. Additional information, advice, or opinions about bank regulations or accounting practices should be obtained from qualified attorneys, accountants, and regulators. The principal regulators for banks and thrifts are:

- The Federal Reserve Board
- Office of the Comptroller of the Currency
- Federal Deposit Insurance Corporation
- Office of Thrift Supervision
- Federal Housing and Finance Board

Other regulators involved in derivatives include:

- Securities and Exchange Commission
- Commodities Futures Trading Commission
- Internal Revenue Service

Federal Reserve Regulations and Policies

Regulations depend on the type of organization (i.e., member of the Federal Reserve, National Bank, state bank, thrifts, credit unions), and the various regulators may differ occasionally on interpretations of requirements. Banks that are members of the Federal Reserve System[3]

1. are generally prohibited from owning stock in any corporation
2. may invest up to 10 percent of their capital and surplus in "investment quality" marketable debt of corporations and other issuers
3. may invest with limitations, and underwrite and deal in securities of other governmental issuers (i.e., U.S. government and its agencies, state and local governments)
4. may enter into futures and options contracts on U.S. government and other specified money market instruments for purposes of reducing their interest rate exposure, but may not enter into them for purposes of speculation.

Bank holding companies (BHCs) are permitted broader securities activities. BHCs are permitted to purchase up to 5 percent of the voting shares in any company, and may take up to 24.9 percent equity interest, as long as they do not control the company. Also, the strict limitations that apply to bank investments do not apply in all respects to BHC investments, with the caveat that the investments meet a standard of prudence. Moreover, the Board of Governors of the Federal Reserve System has (by order) permitted a few bank holding companies to establish securities subsidiaries to underwrite and deal in debt and equity securities.

For example, the Board approved the application of The Sumitomo Bank, Limited (Osaka, Japan), for its wholly owned subsidiary, Sumitomo Bank Capital Markets, Inc. (New York), to act as a dealer, broker, and advisor with respect to interest rate and currency swaps, caps, collars, floors, and related transactions.[4] Sumitomo Bank, Limited, Osaka, is a BHC which also owns Sumitomo Bank of California, Los Angeles. These orders were subject to limitations and conditions that were designed to insulate the bank from its securities affiliates, and to prevent violations of the Glass-Steagall Act.

Certain Federal Reserve policies dealing with financial contracts were written before exchange traded options, swaptions, and other financial instruments and techniques described in this book were created. For example, the Supervisory Policy Statement on Financial Contracts by state member banks was issued jointly by the Fed, the OCC, and the FDIC in 1980.[5] Despite the fact that it is dated, it contains the following statement that applies today:

> Banks that engage in futures, forward and standby contract activities should only do so in accordance with safe and sound banking practices with levels of activity reasonably related to the bank's business needs and capacity to fulfill its obligations under these contracts. In managing their assets and liabilities, banks should evaluate the interest rate risk exposure resulting from their overall activities to ensure that the positions they take in futures, forward, and standby contract markets will reduce their risk exposure; and policy objectives should be formulated in light of the bank's entire asset and liability mix.

High-Risk Mortgage Securities and Similar Products

The Federal Reserve Board issued a revised Supervisory Policy Statement on Securities Activities that became effective on February 10, 1992 (superseding the Policy Statement issued in 1988). The Policy Statement, developed under the auspices of the Federal Financial Institutions Examination Council, applies to banks and other types of federally insured financial institutions.[6] For example, the Policy Statement states that writing covered call options and short sales are not permissible activities for federal credit unions.

The Policy Statement on Securities Activities also addresses mortgage derivative products and zero coupon bonds. Mortgage derivative products include Collateralized Mortgage Obligations (CMOs), Real Estate Investment Conduits (REMICs), CMO and REMIC residuals, and Mortgage-Backed Securities (MBSs). Some MBSs are converted into *interest-only* (IO) strips, where the investor receives the cash flow from interest payments, and *principal-only* (PO) strips, where the investor receives the principal payments and no interest. IOs and POs have highly volatile characteristics due, in part, to the prepayment variability of the underlying mortgages. MBS investors receive cash flow on a pro rata basis. In the case of CMOs and REMICs, however, cash flow is segmented, and paid in accordance with a predetermined priority to investors holding various tranches. *Tranches* are classes or combinations of IO and PO payments, with different stated maturities, estimated average life, coupon rates, and prepayment characteristics. *Residuals* are claims on any excess cash flows from CMOs or other asset-backed securities remaining after the payments due to investors and administrative costs have been met.

Some mortgage derivative products are considered "high-risk," if they meet *any* of the following tests:

1. *Average Life Test.* The expected weighted average life is greater than ten years.

2. *Average Life Sensitivity Test.* Assuming an immediate and sustained parallel shift in the yield curve of 300 basis points, the expected weighted average life of the mortgage derivative product increases by more than four years (decreases by more than six years).

3. *Price Sensitivity Test.* Assuming an immediate and sustained parallel shift in the yield curve of 300 basis points, the price of the mortgage derivative product changes by more than 17 percent.

The general principle is that high-risk mortgage derivative products "are not suitable investments." Having said that, the policy statement makes exceptions to the rule and explains the conditions under which high-risk mortgage securities may be used. "Institutions that hold mortgage derivative products that meet the definition of a high-risk mortgage security must do so to reduce interest rate risk and in accordance with safe and sound practices." The statement goes on to say that the policy statement is not meant to preclude institutions with strong capital and earnings, with adequate liquidity, and with a closely supervised trading department from acquiring high-risk mortgages for trading purposes. Depository institutions that own high-risk mortgage securities must demonstrate the following:

1. A board-approved portfolio policy which addresses the institution's goals and objectives, including interest rate risk reduction objectives with respect to high-risk mortgage securities. The board, or an appropriate committee, must review at least quarterly all high-risk mortgage securities to determine if they are meeting the objectives set forth in the portfolio policy.

2. Limits on the amount of funds that may be committed to high-risk mortgage securities

3. Specific financial officer responsibility and or authority over securities activities involving high-risk mortgage securities

4. An adequate information system

5. Procedures for periodic evaluation of high-risk mortgage securities and their actual performance

6. Appropriate internal controls

Securities and other on- and off-balance sheet products that have characteristics similar to those of high-risk mortgage securities will be subject to the same supervisory treatment as high-risk mortgage securities.

Finally, with respect to long-term zero coupon, stripped, and original issue discount products, the statement states that "disproportionately large holdings of these instruments may be considered an imprudent investment practice, which will be subject to criticism by examiners."

Warning Signs for Directors from the OTS

The Compliance Division of the Office of Thrift Supervision (OTS), U.S. Department of the Treasury, published *Director Information Guidelines* (December, 1989). One part of the document focuses on Asset/Liability Management, and provides "Warning Signs" of impending problems. Although the book is aimed at directors, the warning signs are reproduced here for all readers to heed.

Investment-Portfolio Analysis Warning Signs

- Substantial declines in market value
- Increasing purchases and sales of securities, possibly indicative of unauthorized trading
- Significant shift in the composition of the portfolio toward investments carrying higher credit risk
- Significant shift toward longer-term securities and increasing interest rate risk
- Increasing investment in complex new products that require highly sophisticated and specialized management, such as mortgage derivative securities
- Increasing investment in thinly traded securities

Exposure to Changes in Interest Rate Risk Warning Signs

- Potential for decline in the institution's net interest margin or market value of portfolio equity if interest rates fluctuate beyond established limits
- Past exposure projections that are substantially different from actual operating results

Hedging Warning Signs

- Deviations from the institution's hedging policies and procedures
- Large losses in hedging activities without corresponding gains in assets/liabilities being hedged
- Failure by management to identify precise assets or liabilities being hedged, suggesting that management is speculating rather than hedging
- Excessive transaction costs in relation to the benefits derived from the hedge
- Many buys and sells with little change in net position

Cash Flow/Liquidity Risk Warning Signs

- Increased reliance on volatile funding sources (wholesale deposits) or nontraditional funding sources (asset sales) to meet funding obligations

- Significant variations in cash flows from period to period
- Inability to meet obligations as they become due
- Funds invested in areas new to the institution or in assets with a risk-based capital weighting of 100 percent
- Failure to meet regulatory liquidity requirements

Savings and Core Deposits Warning Signs

- Shift from retail (core) deposits to wholesale (e.g., brokered deposits)
- Shift from longer- to short-term deposits
- Large inflows or outflows to branch offices

Accounting Issues

The foreword to the Financial Accounting Standards Board's (FASB) Research Report, *Hedge Accounting: An Exploratory Study of the Underlying Issues* (1991) points out that although hedging has been going on for hundreds of years, hedge accounting is a relatively recent development.[7] It goes on to define hedge accounting as "a special treatment that ensures that the values of the hedged item and the hedging instrument, from the date the hedge is established, are counterbalanced in the same period(s)."[8] There is a popular saying that something is easier said than done. That statement applies to hedge accounting.

Disclosure and accounting principles have not kept pace with developments in financial innovation. Accordingly, the Organization for Economic Co-operation and Development's (OECD) Working Group on Accounting Standards sponsored a symposium and studies to promote international cooperation in accounting and reporting practices concerning financial innovations. The OECD's *New Financial Instruments* (1991) provides an overview of the FASB's approach to dealing with financial instruments.[9] The FASB projects on financial instruments are broken down into six interrelated parts with the objectives to:

1. Improve disclosure in the notes to financial statements about financial instruments and transactions, including on- and off-balance sheet items, obligations, commitments, and guarantees not now recognized as assets and liabilities
2. Consider whether financial assets should be considered sold if there is recourse with those assets or other involvement with

them. Similarly, whether liabilities should be considered settled if there are assets dedicated to settle them, and other issues relating to non-recognition or offsetting of related assets and liabilities.

3. Consider how hedge instruments used to transfer risk should be accounted for, and how to account for the underlying assets or liabilities being hedged
4. Consider whether financial instruments should be measured at cost, lower of cost or market, or some surrogate for market value
5. Consider how issuers should account for securities that have both debt and equity characteristics
6. Consider what effect separate legal entities, such as joint ventures or special purpose subsidiaries, should have on the recognition of financial instruments and transactions

The OECD described the FASB's view as "global" and "conceptual." For example, the International Accounting Standards Committee (IASC) and the FASB recognize that the term "financial instrument" encompasses a wide variety of instruments, and it requires a consistent definition. Therefore, the IASC has drafted the following definition.[10]

"A financial instrument is any contract that gives rise to both a (recognized or unrecognized) financial asset of one enterprise and a (recognized or unrecognized) financial liability or equity instrument of another enterprise."

Therefore, "a financial asset is any asset that is:

i.   cash;
ii. a contractual right to receive cash or another financial asset from another enterprise;
iii. a contractual right to exchange financial instruments with another enterprise under conditions that are potentially favorable; or
iv. an equity instrument of another enterprise."

"A financial liability is any liability that is a contractual obligation:

i.   to deliver cash or another financial asset to another enterprise; or

ii. to exchange financial instruments with another enterprise under conditions that are potentially unfavorable."

"An equity instrument is any contract that evidences a residual interest in the asset of an enterprise after deducting all of its liabilities."

As a result of these efforts, the FASB issued Statement of Financial Accounting Standards No. 105, *Disclosure of Information about Financial Instruments with Off-Balance Sheet Risk and Financial Instruments with Concentrations of Credit Risk* (March 1990), and Statement of Financial Accounting Standards No. 107, *Disclosures about Fair Value of Financial Instruments* (December 1991). SFAS 105 deals with the disclosure about certain financial instruments. SFAS 107 applies to the disclosure of the fair value financial instruments. Fair value is the amount at which the financial instruments could be exchanged by willing parties in a current transaction, other than in a forced or liquidation sale. The current market price of a financial instrument in an active exchange market is one method of determining fair value. In the case of "custom-tailored" instruments where no active exchange market exists, such as put and call options, models such as the Black-Scholes model or binomial models may be used to determine fair value.

SFAS 105 and 107 apply to financial institutions with assets of $150 million or more. However, bank regulators may require more, or less, from banks of all sizes.

Conclusion

During the 1980s and 1990s, financial innovations and the growth of global financial markets became a reality. The "globalization" of finance forced bank regulators and accounting organizations to take a global perspective with respect to regulations and accounting practices. Thus, it is not surprising that regulations, such as bank capital standards, emanated from the Bank for International Settlements in an effort to strengthen and standardize capital levels of international banks. Similarly, we can expect international regulation of new financial instruments and international financial markets in order to promote safety and soundness. The new financial instruments and global markets create major accounting problems that can only be solved on an international level. The previously cited studies by the OECD and FASB are moves in that direction.

This chapter began with a quote from E. Gerald Corrigan, and it will end with one too. He stated "Off-balance-sheet activities have a role, but they must be managed and controlled carefully, and they must be understood by top management as well as by traders and rocket scientists. They must also be understood by supervisors. In that regard, I can assure you that at both the national and the international level we are redoubling our efforts to ensure that supervisory policies for these activities are sensitive to the full range of risks they present to individual institutions and markets generally."[11]

Endnotes

1. Steven Lipin and William Power, "'Derivatives' Draw Warnings from Regulators," *The Wall Street Journal* (March 25, 1992) C1, C9.

2. BIS statement (January 29, 1992).

3. The author is indebted to Michael J. Schoenfeld, Senior Securities Regulation Analyst, Board of Governors of the Federal Reserve System, for his helpful comments on this subject.

4. Federal Reserve Bulletin (August 1989), 582-585.

5. See Financial Contracts—Policy Statement # 3-1535, Board of Governors of the Federal Reserve System, *Federal Reserve Regulatory Service* 3.478.6-3.479.

6. Other agencies participating in this policy statement are the Federal Deposit Insurance Corporation, the Comptroller of the Currency, National Credit Union Administration, and the Office of Thrift Supervision. The statements presented here are from the Federal Reserve's and OCC's versions of the policy statement. Other agencies' versions may differ somewhat.

7. Harold Bierman, Jr., L. Todd Johnson, and D. Scott Peterson, *Hedge Accounting: An Exploratory Study of the Underlying Issues*, Research Report, Norwalk, Connecticut: Financial Accounting Standards Board (1991).

8. Financial Accounting Standards Board's (FASB) Research Report, *Hedge Accounting: An Exploratory Study of the Underlying Issues* (1991) 216.

9. *New Financial Instruments*, Accounting Standards Harmonization, No. 6. (Paris, France: Organization for Economic Co-operation and Development, 1991). Spelling of some words quoted from this document have been changed to be consistent with usage in the United States.

10. *New Financial Instruments*, 16, 17.

11. E. Gerald Corrigan, "Rebuilding the Economic and Financial Fundamentals: The Case for Vision and Patience," *FRBNY Quarterly Review* (Winter 1991-1992) 5.

INTEREST RATE RISK MANAGEMENT POLICIES

The Comptroller of the Currency Advisory AL 90-1 (January 2, 1990) recognized that the assumption of interest rate risk is an integral part of banking. The advisory went on to say that the OCC is concerned that banks adequately measure and prudently manage interest rate risk, and that capital be available to support that exposure. As part of the OCC's supervision of banks, their examiners will review bank management's policies and results. The examiners are interested in the level of risk and the quality of risk management to determine if the bank has sufficient capital. The four major elements of interest rate risk management are:

- A policy adopted by the board. The interest rate risk management policy may be incorporated into the bank's general fund management policy.
- Measurement of the level of interest risk.
- Limits on the amount of interest rate risk that the bank will take.
- Regular reports to management and to the board.

Interest rate risk management policies and practices vary from bank to bank, depending on their particular circumstances. Nevertheless, it is instructive to study the policies of different banks. The remainder of this chapter consists of excerpts of policies from two medium-sized commercial banks ($300 million in assets), one large bank holding company ($5 billion in assets), and policies used by Federal Home Loan Banks. The two medium-sized banks allow us to observe differences between two banks of about the same size. The policies of the large bank holding company reflect a more sophisticated use of interest rate risk management techniques than those of the medium-sized banks. The policies of the Federal Home Loan Banks provide clues about how one federal regulatory agency manages its own funds. These excerpts and policies are presented solely for purposes of illustration.

Medium-Sized Bank A (MSBA)
$300 Million in Assets
Funds Management Policy

Overview

As the rate environment in which commercial banks operate continues to remain volatile, and with the increased competition for both deposit dollars and quality investments, it has become increasingly difficult to maintain the desired interest rate spreads. With the outlook for interest rate trends and increased competition remaining unchanged, it is of primary importance that the bank manage both the assets and liabilities for adequate funding, maximum spread, and minimal interest rate exposure.

I. Purpose

The purpose of the Funds Management Policy of MSBA will be to act as a guide for profit planning as well as to establish asset/liability management communications and control procedures. These procedures will include liquidity and capital planning, asset mix and volume controls, loans and deposit pricing policies, and investment portfolio strategies.

II. Policy and Procedures

Funds Management is a direct result of the bank's efforts to maintain soundness and profitability for the long term. A summary of the long-range plans and objectives is as follows:

A. General Goal:

1. To preserve the integrity and safety of the deposits and capital base of the bank.
2. To attain and sustain a strong level of earnings as further protection for our depositors and to assure an appropriate return to our stockholders on their investment.
3. To be an asset to our market area and, within our capacity, to be responsive to the needs of our market area.

B. Specific Goals and Procedures

1. Establish a Funds Management Committee which will establish and monitor the volume and mix of the bank's assets and funding sources to produce results that are consistent with the bank's liquidity, capital adequacy, growth, risk, and profitability goals. The committee will be duly established with the Board of Directors' approval and will meet on a monthly basis. Minutes of each meeting will be taken and reported to the Board quarterly. The committee will be chaired by the Chief Executive Officer, and will consist of the President, the Senior Vice President of Commercial Loans, the Senior Vice President of Operations, a Vice President of Commercial Loans to serve as the Funds Management Officer and the Loan Review Officer. Other officers will be invited from time to time. The President or Funds Management Officer will direct the meetings in the absence of the Chief Executive Officer. The bank's Loan Review Officer will act as Secretary to the Committee.

In conjunction with the most recent rate sensitivity information on the bank, the committee should review the following information:

   a. Local and national business and economic conditions

   b. Forecast for changes in interest rates

   c. Anticipated changes in the volume and mix of the loan and investment portfolios

   d. Anticipated changes in the volume and mix of the bank's sources of funding

   e. A comparative presentation of key bank performance ratios

   f. Any changes that need to be made to the Funds Management Policy

   g. Anticipated changes in the volume and mix of the bank's sources of funds (Fed Funds, Large CDs, Demand Deposits, Money Market Deposits, and other Time Deposits)

   h. The bank's dependence on Fed Funds purchased, jumbo CDs, Repos, Public Funds

   i. The maturity distribution of assets and liabilities

   j. Year-to-date bank operating results, and the bank's plan for the rest of the year

     k. Alternative sources of funds

     l. Cash and due from balances

     m. Tax strategies

     n. Current loan strategies, investment strategies, and funding strategies

2. The current rates being offered by the bank on deposit accounts and loan pricing should be reviewed and adjusted if necessary.

3. The liquidity ratio is measured by net liquid assets to net liability and should be calculated on a monthly basis. This ratio should be maintained at a level of at least 20 percent. In addition, secondary liquidity will be reviewed monthly. Items to be reviewed in secondary liquidity include federal funds, credit lines, possible loan participations, Federal Reserve borrowings, and unpledged, nonliquid investments.

4. Maintain a total equity capital to total assets ratio of at least 7 percent, including the loan loss reserve. This will allow the bank to be adequately protected against risk of loss in the loan or investment portfolio. The loan to deposit ratio will not exceed 100 percent.

5. Rate sensitivity should be monitored and strategies developed to adjust the sensitivity as the rate environment dictates. The desired levels are as follows:

$$\frac{\text{RATE SENSITIVE ASSETS}}{\text{RATE SENSITIVE LIABILITIES}} \quad \text{for 0-90 days should range between 85 percent \& 115 percent}$$

$$\frac{\text{RATE SENSITIVE ASSETS}}{\text{RATE SENSITIVE LIABILITIES}} \quad \text{for 90-180 days should range between 85 percent \& 115 percent}$$

$$\frac{\text{RATE SENSITIVE ASSETS}}{\text{RATE SENSITIVE LIABILITIES}} \quad \text{for 180-365 days should range between 85 percent \& 115 percent}$$

Any deviation from the above levels will be carefully scrutinized by the committee.

6. The bank will use all sources of deposits available to fund operations, with the exception of brokered deposits.

7. The tax position of the bank should be managed to provide the maximum benefit to the stockholders on a consistent basis. The

committee will review quarterly the anticipated tax liability to determine the usefulness of tax-exempt securities and other legitimate tax shelters.

In summary, the goal of the bank is to maintain consistent earnings which are independent of the fluctuations of the business cycle.

Medium-Sized Bank B (MSBB)
$300 Million in Assets

Membership of the Asset Liability Management Committee (ALCO)

Standing members of the ALCO will consist of individuals representing the following positions:

- Chair of the Board and Chief Executive Officer (CEO)
- Vice Chair of the Board and Executive Financial Officer (EFO)
- Executive Vice President and Comptroller
- Executive Vice President/Retail Banking
- Executive Vice President/Corporate Banking
- Executive Vice President/Investments
- Senior Vice President/Compliance
- Assistant Corporate Comptroller
- Deposit Product Manager

The Executive Financial Officer shall serve as Chair. A member of the committee or other staff shall be named to serve as Secretary of the committee.

Duties of the ALCO

During its meetings the ALCO members will review:

1. Minutes of the previous meeting.
2. Ratio of the amount of rate sensitive assets to the amount of rate sensitive liabilities, which are sensitive within defined time frames. The ALCO will also review funds gap reports, which itemize rate sensitive assets and rate sensitive liabilities and their maturity distributions. Furthermore, the ALCO will review

rate sensitivity reports as well as mix/spread analyses to assess the effects of anticipated changes in interest rates, and of the volume and mix of asset and liability items on net interest margin.

3. Alternative scenarios developed through sensitivity or "what if" analyses. These scenarios will incorporate such variables as loan demand, investment opportunities, core deposit growth, regulatory changes, monetary policy adjustments, the overall state of the economy, and interest rates on particular sources and uses of funds.

4. Current commercial and consumer base rates, which are designed to ensure that loans are priced in accordance with the overall loan strategy.

5. Current liability and deposit pricing matrixes, which are designed to ensure that funds are priced in accordance with overall funding strategies.

6. Maturity distribution of the certificate of deposit portfolio.

7. Results of the implementation of funding strategies, which are designed to ensure that the bank has adequate funds for loans, investments, deposits and debt repayment.

8. Current and prospective liquidity position, considering both assets and liabilities.

9. Prospective assessment of the accessibility of funds—both for shorter-term and capital purposes—at a price that will give a reasonable and consistent return on investment in relation to the risk involved.

Discussion of information, recommendations, and actions taken by the ALCO will be recorded in the minutes of the meeting. Copies of these minutes will be distributed to the ALCO members and other key personnel; a copy of the minutes for each meeting will be maintained on file.

Liquidity Policy

Maintenance of a sufficient level of liquidity shall be a primary objective of the ALCO. Liquidity shall be defined as the ability to meet anticipated and unanticipated operating cash needs, loan demand, and deposit withdrawals, without incurring a sustained negative impact on profitability.

Target levels for loans to deposits are in the 70 percent to 80 percent range, and for loans to core deposits are in the 80 percent to 90 percent range. These ratios are reported on the monthly financial management report, and the ALCO will refer to this report to monitor them. Deviations from these targets will trigger discussion of the possibility of corrective action.

Interest Risk Policy

MSBB's goal is to minimize risk and earnings vulnerability due to increases and decreases in external market rates. The committee will review various analyses and models, and take appropriate actions to meet this goal. The committee will attempt to maintain the six-month and one-year cumulative ratios of rate sensitive assets to rate sensitive liabilities between 0.9 and 1.1. Hedging or swap activities will be considered in the achievement of this goal. If this ratio exceeds 1.15 or falls below 0.85, specific plans must be formulated to bring it back in line or, alternatively, this policy may be reviewed.

The method used in computing these gap ratios is based on MSBB's recent rate sensitivity experience and is more indicative than the methods prescribed by regulatory reporting requirements. For this reason, the gap ratios used by the ALCO may differ from gap ratios disclosed in regulatory and stockholder reports.

Planning models will be run, testing earnings vulnerability to different, reasonably plausible, interest rate scenarios. If these models indicate a potential earnings effect of ten percent or more, then the committee shall formulate plans to mitigate this potential problem.

Board and Management Reporting

The EFO will make reports to management, the ALCO, and the bank's board of directors as needed.

Policy Exceptions

This policy is intended to be flexible to deal with rapidly changing conditions, and, as such, can be amended with the approval of the board. Exceptions to the policy may be made only with the approval of the CEO and ALCO or, in the absence of a quorum, the CEO.

Large Bank Holding Company (LBHC)
$5 Billion in Assets

Purpose

The Asset/Liability Management Policy encompasses overall management of LBHC and all affiliates' balance sheets; and specific management of investment assets, purchased liabilities, and off-balance sheet transactions related to the management of interest rate risk.

The objective of the Asset/Liability Management Policy is to direct management in the acquisition and deployment of funds for both on- and off-balance sheet exposure, while optimizing net interest income within the constraints of prudent capital adequacy, liquidity, and safety.

The Asset/Liability Management Policy strives to keep LBHC focused in the future, anticipating and exploring alternatives, rather than simply reacting to change after the fact. This policy must maintain balance between sufficient guidance to encourage management to adhere to sound fundamentals of banking and flexibility to exercise the creativity and innovations necessary to meet the challenges in the market.

The management of LBHC seeks to maximize shareholder value by improving current income while protecting the earning stream from interest rate shocks. The corporate earnings objectives are 16 percent ROE and 10 percent EPS growth.

Authority

The operating responsibility for implementing, interpreting, and maintaining this policy shall reside with the Asset/Liability Committee (ALCO). The Asset/Liability Committee has been given its authority by the board of directors. Prudent asset/liability management requires coordination and evaluation from a broad corporate perspective; therefore, this policy establishes minimum requirements and action guidelines necessary to foster and assure proper coordination throughout the bank, while striving to reach objectives.

Compliance

This policy and all other policies listed are in full compliance with all state and federal laws, rules, and regulations.

Leverage

The amount of legally available leverage is reported to the ALCO. The ALCO decides how much of the available leverage will be used.

The ALCO will meet at least monthly. The ALCO shall require whatever reporting necessary to remain apprised of activities undertaken by operating management, to ensure continued compliance with the guidelines it establishes and with the policies of the Board of Directors.

Policies

The ALCO shall establish and maintain formal operating guidelines to provide management with the framework and constraints for day-to-day decision-making. The Correspondent and Investment Services Division of LBHC will be responsible for the following policies:

1. Asset/Liability Management
2. Interest Rate Risk
3. Investment
4. Funding
5. Liquidity
6. Investment Banking Division

All of these policies should be reviewed and approved by the ALCO annually. Any exceptions to these policies must be reported to the ALCO at the first scheduled opportunity or in memo form.

Addendum

The addendum by bank includes ALCO members, quorum requirements, and reports reviewed regularly.

Interest Rate Risk Management Policy

Purpose

The interest rate risk policy establishes minimum requirements and guidelines for monitoring and controlling the level and amount of interest rate risk. This policy describes methods employed by LBHC for measuring the present and future risks associated with changes in interest rates.

The objective of the interest rate risk policy is to direct management to project, evaluate and manage the impact of interest rate risk on LBHC's earnings.

Changes in interest rates may have a material effect on LBHC's earnings and market value. The degree of risk depends upon such factors as the maturity structure and repricing frequency of balance sheet cash flows, customer prepayments or refinancing, lending, and funding strategies.

The management of interest rate risk, by definition, means either reducing or increasing the level of risk exposure. The level of risk can be managed directly by changing the repricing and maturity characteristics of the cash flows for specific assets or liabilities. Changing these characteristics can be accomplished in the cash markets, or on balance sheet, or off balance sheet by options, futures, swaps, caps or floors.

To successfully manage interest rate risk, LBHC must first employ methods with which to monitor existing interest rate exposure. Simulation modeling, rate sensitivity and duration are measurement techniques used. Measurements based on assumptions as to the interest rate sensitivity and repricing characteristics of cash flows for each asset and liability shall provide the foundation by which management shall monitor and control interest rate risk exposure.

Results of these measures will aid management in the development and implementation of strategies that minimize exposure to interest rate risk and ensure stable and consistent earnings growth.

Administration

It shall be the responsibility of the ALCO to monitor ongoing interest rate risk management activities and review proposed strategies presented by the Correspondent and Investment Services Division of LBHC. The asset/liability area of the CISD of LBHC shall be responsible for reporting the results of specific measures that provide information concerning existing exposure to interest rate risk.

Model Simulations

Management has concluded that simulation modeling is the most beneficial measure of interest rate risk. It is a dynamic measure. By employing a simulation process that measures the impact of forecasted changes in interest rates and balance sheet structures and establishing limits on changes in net interest income, management is able to evaluate the potential risks associated with alternative strategies.

The asset/liability area shall prepare a base balance sheet and income statement simulation. The base case simulation shall represent current balance sheet growth trends projected forward. Base case simulation results will be prepared under a flat interest rate forecast and at least two alternative interest rate forecasts, one rising and one declining, assuming parallel yield curve shifts.

Comparisons showing the earnings variance from the flat rate forecast illustrate the risks associated with the current balance sheet strategy.

When necessary, additional balance sheet strategies shall be developed and simulations prepared under the same interest rate forecasts used with the base case simulation and nonparallel yield curve shifts. These additional strategies will be used to measure yield curve risk, prepayment risk, basis risk, and index lag risk inherent in the balance sheet. Comparisons showing the earnings variance from the base case provide management with information concerning the risks associated with implementing the alternative strategies.

To effectively evaluate results from model simulations, limits on the change in net interest income shall be established by which comparisons can be made. Management has determined that for every 100 basis point (1%) change in interest rates no more than a 5 percent (5%) change in annual net interest income shall occur. Review of results from model simulations will indicate whether current interest rate risk strategies provide adequate protection and, if not, what alternative strategies might.

Assumptions regarding the repricing characteristics of specific assets and liabilities are necessary in preparing model simulations. These assumptions include:

1. An amortization schedule for fixed-rate installment loans based on assumed weighted average maturity (WAM) calculated from the installment loan system reports.

2. Amortization schedules and prepayments for investment securities based on an assumed WAM and assumptions regarding prepayment speeds.

3. Monthly average balances can be used when the ending balance of an asset or liability is historically erratic. Examples are: Fed funds sold, trading account assets, repurchase or reverse repurchase

agreements, cash and due from, demand deposits, other assets, or other liabilities.

4. Since model simulation uses a mixture of actual and average balances, the difference between total assets and total liabilities and equity is considered Fed funds purchased/sold.

Analysis of Rate Sensitivity

The measure for the overall interest rate sensitivity position is the "gap." The Analysis of Rate Sensitivity report (gap report) is designed to show the overall interest sensitivity of the balance sheet, including the impact from off-balance sheet transactions. The gap report allows management to view the exposure to interest rate risk at different time periods. Period-end and cumulative gap positions, or the difference between asset balances repricing and liabilities repricing, and the ratio of cumulative assets repricing to cumulative liabilities repricing are calculated and compared to earning assets.

Management has determined that the 90-day, 180-day and one-year gap positions are the most important time periods to view interest rate risk exposure. Based on historical trends and performance, management has determined that the ratio of gap to earning assets should be within the range of plus or minus 15 percent in one year.

For the gap report to more accurately reflect the interest rate sensitivity of the balance sheet, assumptions as to repricing characteristics of certain assets and liabilities have been made. These assumptions include the following:

1. Fixed rate installment and consumer real estate loans are classified based on an assumed amortization schedule.

2. Investment securities that are subject to prepayments and amortization of principal are classified based on assumptions regarding both.

3. Monthly average balances are used when the ending balance of the asset or liability historically is erratic. Examples are: Fed funds sold, trading account assets, repurchase or revere repurchase agreements, cash and due from, demand deposits, other assets, or other liabilities.

4. Savings NOW, and other long-term time account balances are considered fixed rate and are classified in the over-five-year repricing time period.

5. Rates on rate sensitive accounts and checking accounts are tied to changes in the prime rate and consequently are classified in the immediately repriceable time period.

6. Demand deposits are considered non-rate sensitive and classified in the over-five-year repricing time period. When calculating duration and market value, ranges of assumptions are used regarding the rate sensitivity of demand deposits.

7. Stockholders' equity is considered non-rate sensitive and classified in the over-five-year repricing time period. When calculating duration and market value, ranges of assumptions are used regarding the rate sensitivity of equity.

8. Since the gap report uses a mixture of actual and average balances, the difference between total assets and total liabilities and equity is considered Fed funds purchased/sold.

It shall be the responsibility of the asset/liability area to prepare the Analysis of Rate Sensitivity report and present the results to ALCO. The Correspondent and Investment Services Division shall be responsible for developing alternative strategies that correct gap positions that are not within acceptable limits or improve existing gap positions.

Although the gap report provides management with a method of measuring current interest rate risk, the report is extremely limited in that it is "static" in nature, meaning it only measures the rate sensitivity at a specific point in time. Recognition is given to the limitations of this report.

It is possible for model simulations and gaps to conflict. It is management's opinion that model simulations are more accurate and more beneficial in managing interest rate risk for the organization.

Duration and Market Value Analysis

Duration measures the cash flows from a financial instrument and weights them according to when they are received. In a slightly modified form, duration can be used to approximate changes in market value of individual portfolios or the total balance sheet for movements in interest rates. Use of duration calculations shall provide management with a starting point by which to measure the impact on the market value of stockholders' equity from changes in interest rates.

The following excerpts were taken from the Federal Housing Finance Board's Financial Management Policy, which may be used by all of the Federal Home Loan Banks. Individual Federal Home Loan Banks, such as FHL Bank of Topeka, have adopted their own policies. Federal Home Loan banks, like commercial banks and thrifts, must deal with interest rate risk.

Federal Housing Finance Board
1991
Financial Management Policy
for the Federal Home Loan Bank System

Preamble

The Financial Management Policy for the Federal Home Loan Bank System is being established by the Federal Housing Finance Board to provide guidance to, and establish limits for, the Federal Home Loan Banks (FHLBanks or "Banks") in their development and implementation of financial programs and strategies. This Policy is designed to allow the FHLBanks to implement prudent financial management strategies to accomplish their housing finance mission in a safe, sound, and profitable manner.

IV. Hedge Transaction Guidelines

A. **Purpose:** To allow implementation of hedge programs that control the interest rate or basis risk which arises in the ordinary course of operation.

B. **Authorized Strategies:** Long and short positions in the cash, forward, futures, and option markets (including caps and floors), and the purchase and sale of interest rate exchange agreements (swaps), are authorized if they reduce the interest rate or basis risk exposure to which the Federal Home Loan Banks are subjected in their normal course of business. Speculative use of instruments and transactions authorized for hedging purposes is not permitted. Hedging strategies utilizing approved instruments may be implemented so long as the specific objectives are explicitly stated at the time of execution, adequate documentation is maintained during the life of the hedge, and the hedge is designed to:

1. Reduce the interest rate, basis, or option risk associated with consolidated bonds, discount notes and other liabilities; advances or commitments for advances; or investments.

2. Enable a Bank to comply with the limitations established for interest rate risk in section VI of this Policy.

C. **Hedging with Interest Rate Exchange Agreements (Swaps) and Options** (Including Caps and Floors):

1. If a Bank enters into any swap or option agreement that may require future payments to be made to the Bank, the counterparty (including any member counterparty) or its guarantor shall be a highly rated institution, or the obligation shall be adequately secured in accordance with the minimum collateralization requirements (subsection IV.C.6).

2. A Bank may enter into an unsecured interest rate swap or option agreement with a counterparty that does not meet the minimum credit standards as long as the transaction results in a reduction of credit risk arising from previously existing swap or option agreements with that counterparty.

3. Unsecured risk exposure associated with interest rate swaps and options is governed by the Unsecured Credit Guidelines (section V of this Policy).

4. A Bank may, for hedging purposes, enter into interest rate swap agreements in which the notional principal balance amortizes based upon the prepayment experience of a specified group of mortgage backed securities or the behavior of an interest rate index (Indexed Principal Swaps), or swap agreements which may be terminated or extended at the option of the Bank or its counterparty (swaptions).

   a. Interest rate swaps that amortize according to the behavior of Interest-Only or Principal-Only stripped mortgage backed securities are prohibited.

   b. Interest rate swaps that amortize according to the behavior of residual interest accrual classes of CMOs or REMICs are prohibited.

   c. Indexed principal swaps that have average lives that vary by more than six years under an assumed instantaneous change in interest rates of 300 basis points from the estimated base case are prohibited.

d. The aggregate notional principal amount of indexed principal swaps and swaptions shall not exceed 100 percent of a Bank's capital on the trade date of the transaction.

5. In addition to interest rate caps and floors, a Bank may take long and short hedge positions in any options contract provided that:

   a. The underlying instrument is either a security authorized for investment by this policy or a futures contract authorized by this policy.

   b. The hedge is constructed in a manner such that the price volatility of the option position is consistent with the price volatility of the cash instrument being hedged or the option component of that instrument.

   c. The option contract is traded on an organized exchange regulated by the Commodities Futures Trading Commission or the Securities and Exchange Commission; or through a recognized securities dealer which reports its position regularly to the Federal Reserve Bank of New York.

6. Collateral Security: A Bank shall require collateral for interest rate swaps and options from those counterparties (or guarantors) that do not meet the definition of highly rated institutions and for credit risk exposure that exceeds established limits on unsecured extensions of credit on the trade date of the transaction. The dollar amount of collateral shall be maintained in accordance with the requirements of the Bank's agreement with the counterparty and shall be determined by the Bank commensurate with the risk undertaken, but shall be no less than the following minimum levels:

   a. For a fixed/floating swap or a floating/fixed swap, a minimum initial collateral maintenance level must be established that is no less than 0.5 percent of the notional amount. Collateral required during the life of the transactions will be no less than the market value of the swap, plus net accrued interest due to the Bank, plus 0.5 percent of the notional amount. The collateral required will be no less than zero (0) for all transactions with a counterparty governed by the same master contract. For floating/floating (basis) swaps, collateral must be maintained sufficient to compensate for the difference in the volatility of the indices.

b. Each Bank may, at its discretion, waive collateral requirements for member swaps that are matched to collateralized advances, or offsetting swaps, as long as the matching advances, or offsetting swaps, are outstanding.

c. For option transactions in which the Bank is a potential receiver of payments, a minimum initial collateral maintenance level must be established that is no less than the market value of the contract, plus 0.5 percent of the transaction amount.

7. Documentation:

a. Market value determinations and subsequent collateral adjustments should be made, at a minimum, on a monthly basis.

b. Failure to meet a collateral call shall result in an early termination event.

c. Early termination pricing and methodology shall be detailed in all interest rate swap and option contracts in which a Bank is involved as principal. This methodology must reflect a reasonable estimate of the market value of the swap or option at termination.

d. The transfer of an agreement or contract by a counterparty shall be made only with the consent of the Bank.

e. Transactions with a single counterparty shall be governed by a single master agreement when practicable.

8. Non-U.S. dollar denominated swaps are authorized only to convert matching non-dollar denominated debt to dollar denominated debt, or to offset another non-dollar denominated swap.

D. Hedging in the Financial Futures Markets:

1. Long and short positions in financial futures may be used for hedging provided that:

a. The underlying instrument in an investment or transaction that is eligible under this policy.

b. The price of the futures contract has a high correlation with the price of the cash instrument being hedged.

c. The futures contract is traded on an organized exchange regulated by the Commodities Futures Trading Commission.

d. If delivery of the underlying security will place the Bank in a position of exceeding any investment limitation set by this Policy, the Bank must close out the position prior to taking delivery.

e. Any Bank with a position which exceeds 5 percent of the open interest in any specific futures contract month shall report that position to the investment desks of the other Banks and to the Finance Board within one business day of the initiation of the position. Notification shall also be provided when such a position declines below 5 percent.

E. **Hedging in the Cash or Forward Markets:**

1. The purchase or sale of cash market securities for either regular (cash) or forward delivery is permitted, provided that:

   a. Only securities authorized under the Investment Guidelines section of this policy are used.

   b. The price of the cash or forward instrument has a high correlation with the price of the instrument being hedged.

   c. Any security purchased in the cash market for hedging purposes is included in the investment limits of this Policy.

2. Short positions in instruments authorized in this Policy, the purchase of securities under resale agreements, and the borrowing of securities in connection with short sales is authorized for hedging purposes.

VI. Interest Rate Risk Guidelines

A. **Purpose:** To set prudent limits on the extent to which each Bank may be exposed to interest rate risk.

B. **Interest Rate Risk Limitation:**

1. Each Bank is required to maintain the duration of its equity (at current interest rate levels using the consolidated obligations cost curve) within a range of +5 years to –5 years.

2. Each Bank is required to maintain its duration of equity, under an assumed 200 basis point change in interest rates, within a range of +7 years to –7 years.

3. Duration of equity calculations shall be performed by the Finance Board based upon data supplied by the Banks at intervals prescribed by the Finance Board. Banks which have internal duration models may submit their results, if different from those calculated by the Finance Board, to evidence compliance with this policy. Determination of compliance will ultimately rest with the Finance Board.

Glossary

This glossary contains many words and expressions that are used in connection with asset/liability management and derivative securities. The definitions presented here are those used in the context of ALM and derivative securities. Words that are *italicized* are explained elsewhere in this section.

Advanced settled An *interest rate swap* in which the cash exchanges are made as soon as the floating rate is set.

American-style An *option* which allows the holder to exercise on or before the *maturity date*.

Amortizing swap The *notional principal* on the swap is amortized over the life of the swap. Many loans are amortized, resulting in demand for swap *notional principal* to also be amortized.

Anticipatory hedge A *long* hedge is also called an anticipatory hedge because the hedger anticipates buying the cash commodity.

Asset/liability management (ALM) Managing both assets and liabilities simultaneously for the purpose of mitigating interest rate risk, providing liquidity, and to enhance the value of *banks*.

Asymmetric hedge A technique used in managing interest rate risk where *rate sensitive assets* and *rate sensitive liabilities* are unequal. This type of hedge provides a variable spread between returns on assets and interest costs resulting in increases or decreases in *net interest income* and the value of the bank.

At-the-money At-the-money options are where the *strike price* just equals the value of the underlying item.

Averaged options Averaged options are similar to the standard *options* in *caps* and *floors* except the floating rate is based on an average rate. Averaged options mitigate the risk that the interest rate on the *reset date* is atypical.

Banks We use the term "bank" as a matter of convenience to include all financial institutions or other organizations that are faced with interest rate risk.

Basis The basis refers to the spread between the cash price and the futures price, which may be positive, zero, or negative.

Basis point A basis point is 1/100 of one percentage point, or 0.0001 (or 0.01%), and is used in quoting bonds and other prices. **Basis point value (BPV)** is the dollar change in a debt security in response to a one-basis-point change in the value of that security.

Basis swap The swap is between two floating interest rates. The need for a basis swap arises when your assets and liabilities are both floating, but the floating rate is pegged to different interest rates such as Treasury bills and Eurodollars.

Bond A long-term credit instrument that contains a promise to pay both principal and interest on a loan on predetermined dates. However, some bonds pay no interest (zero coupon), and others never pay the principal amount (perpetuals). Therefore, it is difficult to capture the meaning of a bond in one definition because there are so many exceptions. The face value of most bonds is $1000. The term *discount* means that the bond is selling below face value, and the term *premium* means that it is selling above face value.

Call option An *option* giving the holder the right to buy an item (such as a common stock) at a stated price before a stated time.

Cap An interest rate cap is a financial arrangement that limits the exposure of a floating rate borrower to upward movements in interest rates. A cap is a series of interest rate *call options* in which the writer guarantees the buyer that he will pay the buyer whatever additional interest he must pay on his loan if the rate on that loan goes above an agreed rate.

Captions Captions are *options* on a cap. That is, you buy an option to buy a cap, which itself is a portfolio of options on interest rates. Thus, captions are options on a portfolio of options.

Cash market The price of a commodity for immediate delivery (same or next-day).

Cheapest-to-deliver As a result of variation in prices among bonds that are qualified to be delivered under a *futures contract*, sellers select the one that is cheapest to deliver. Also see *conversion factor*.

Circus swap The swap involves currencies as well as interest rates. This type of swap is useful when managing both currency risk and interest rate risk simultaneously. This swap is most appropriate for multinational banks.

Closing transaction The closing transaction is any purchase or sale where an already established position is offset.

Collar An interest rate collar is just the combination of a *cap* and a *floor*. An interest rate collar is a financial arrangement combining caps and floors that limits a floating rate loan payment on both the upward side (cap) and on the downward side (floor). A collar is just short a cap and long a floor (or vice versa).

Collateralized mortgage obligations (CMOs) These are *derivative securities* created from mortgage-backed bonds, primarily issued by the Federal National Mortgage Association and the Federal Home Loan Mortgage Association.

Commodity As used here, commodities refer to those items of trade that underlie *futures contracts*, such as grains, financial instruments, currencies, stock indexes, and so on.

Conversion factor Conversion factors are used to adjust the principal invoice prices of those bonds with coupons and maturities that differ from the standard used in a *futures contract*.

Counterparties The buyers and sellers involved in FRAs are referred to as counterparties. One counterparty to the FRA will receive a fixed interest payment and pay a floating interest payment. The other counterparty to the FRA will receive a floating interest payment and pay a fixed interest payment.

Credit risk Credit risk on a swap is the risk that the *counterparty* fails to perform as the counterparty is contractually bound. The loss exposure is the cost of replacing the swap when it has positive value.

Cross hedge This refers to *hedging* a cash market risk in one *commodity* (security) with a *futures contract* in a different, but related commodity (security).

Cumulative gap See *periodic gap*.

Default risk U.S. Treasury securities are risk-free. *Risk-free* means that they have no default risk—the interest and principal will be paid by the Treasury.

Deferred (forward) swap The swap does not begin until a later date. This type of swap is appropriate for a bank with no *gap* problem in the short maturity range, but increasing disparity for longer maturities.

Derivative securities Derivative securities are derived (created) from previously existing securities. *Put* and *call options*, mortgage backed securities, and swaps are examples of derivative securities. They derive their value from the value of the underlying stock, mortgage, or cash flow.

Discount The face value of most *bonds* is $1,000. The term *discount* means that the bond is selling below face value, and the term *premium* means that it is selling above face value.

Duration The weighted average term to maturity of all cash flows received from an investment such as a bond, assets, or liabilities. Duration depends, in part, on maturity.

Duration drift The drift occurs with the passage of time; the duration gets shorter as the bond approaches maturity. See *gap*.

European-style An *option* which the holder can only *exercise* on the *maturity date*.

Exercise The act of the holder to render the *option* contract to purchase (sell) the underlying item at the strike price for calls (puts).

Exercise price See *strike price*.

Expectations theory This theory postulates that long-term interest rates are an average of intervening short-term rates. In addition, investors are indifferent about choosing between holding long-term or short-term debt securities (bonds), as long as they obtain their required rate of return. The return that they expect to receive depends mostly on the price of the bonds.

Expiration date See *maturity date*.

Extendable swap One *counterparty* to the swap has the right to lengthen the swap. This feature adds flexibility to the swap holder, allowing the holder to extend the life of the swap if necessary.

Financial futures Financial futures are *futures contracts* on financial instruments.

Financing bias The financing bias refers to the slight pricing differences which develop due to interest rate *forward contracts* not being *marked-to-market*, whereas futures contracts are marked-to-market daily.

Fixed rate payer The *counterparty* to a swap, which pays based on the fixed rate and receives based on the floating rate.

Floating interest payment The floating interest payment is set on the *reset date*, which is specified in the FRA.

Floating rate payer The *counterparty* to a swap which pays based on the floating rate and receives based on the fixed rate.

Floor An interest rate floor is a financial arrangement that limits the exposure of a floating rate lender to downward movements in interest rates. A floor is a series of interest rate *put options*; the *writer* guarantees the interest she must pay on her loan if the rate on that loan goes below an agreed rate.

Floortions Floortions are *options* on a *floor*.

Foreign exchange risk The risk that there will be adverse changes in foreign exchange rates.

Forward contract A forward contract is a contract between a buyer and a seller to trade something in the future at a price negotiated today. A forward contract is obligatory to both the buyer and the seller.

Forward rate agreement (FRA) A *forward contract* on interest rates.

Futures contract A futures contract is a marketable *forward contract*. A futures contract is an agreement to make delivery (*short*) at a later date or to accept delivery (*long*) of a fixed amount of a specific quality of an asset at a specified price.
These contracts give the holder the right to buy or sell the underlying *commodity* at specified price on a specified date. The contract specifications vary from commodity to commodity. Futures contracts are traded on organized commodity exchanges.

Gap In banking jargon, *gap* is the difference between *rate sensitive assets* and *rate sensitive liabilities* expressed in dollars. Gap can also be measured in terms of *duration*. See *periodic gap*.

Hedging is a technique used to transfer risk. The technical definition of *hedging* is "the initiation of a position in the futures market that is intended as a temporary substitute for the sale or purchase of the actual commodity."

Holding period The return on investment (income and price changes) for a given period of time.

Immunization The use of *duration* to obtain a realized yield that will not be less than the *yield to maturity* for that *holding period* at the time the investments were made.

Income risk Income risk refers to the risk of losing income when movements in borrowing and lending rates are not perfectly synchronized. In banking jargon, it is a *gap* problem that arises when there is a mismatch, in terms of time and interest rates, between repricing both assets and liabilities.

Inflation premium See *real interest rate*.

Interest The price paid for the use of credit.

Interest only (IOs) See *stripping*.

Interest rate repricing Interest rate repricing refers to the time when the interest rate on an instrument is adjusted.

Interest rate risk The Canada Deposit Insurance Corporation defines interest rate risk as follows: "Interest rate risk is the potential impact on a member's earnings and net asset values of changes in interest rates. Interest rate risk arises when an institution's principal and interest cash flows (including final maturities), both on- and off-balance sheet, have mismatched pricing dates. The amount of risk is a function of the magnitude and direction of interest rate changes and the size and maturity of the mismatch positions." Also see *investment risk* and *income risk*.

Interest rate swap An interest rate swap is a contract between two *counterparties* who agree to exchange an interest payment based on a *notional principal* tied to a floating rate, in exchange for an interest payment tied to a fixed rate.

In-the-money An in-the-money *option* is one where *exercising* the option now would generate a profit (ignoring the purchase price). That is, for *calls* an option is in-the-money if the underlying item is greater than the *strike price*. For *puts* an option is in-the-money if the underlying item is less than the strike price.

Intrinsic value The intrinsic value of an *option* is zero, or the dollar amount that the underlying asset is *in-the-money*, whichever is greater. The intrinsic value is the value of the *option* if it were immediately *exercised*.

Investment risk Investment risk arises when changes in interest rates cause changes in the market value of fixed-rate and off-balance sheet items. Investment risk is sometimes called *price risk*.

Law of one price The law of one price states that portfolios with identical future cash flows should trade at the same price today.

Long Buying or owning an asset. The holder of the *option*, the option buyer, is said to be long.

Margin Margin is a good faith deposit for commodities transactions. It also refers to the credit extended to buy stocks and bonds.

Margin deposit A margin deposit is a good faith deposit to guarantee performance on the contract, usually 3 to 10 percent of the contract value.

Marked-to-market *Futures contracts* are marked-to-market, which means profits and losses are taken daily based on the change in *settlement prices*.

Maturity buckets See *periodic gap*.

Maturity date The date when the swap matures, the last day on which interest accrues. Alternatively, the date on which an *option* contract matures. An option holder after this date has no rights under the contract.

Moneyness Refers to the difference (whether positive or negative) between the price of the underlying asset and the strike price.

Net interest income (NII) Interest income minus interest expense.

Nominal interest rate See *real interest rate*.

Notional principal The notional principal is the amount on which interest payments for a swap are calculated, for example, $1 million. At no time does the $1 million actually trade hands.

Offsetting A sale of an identical previous purchase is offsetting. Alternatively, a purchase of an identical previous sale is offsetting.

Open interest Open interest is the number of *futures contracts* that exist at any point in time.

Opening transaction The opening transaction is any purchase or sale where a new position is established.

Option A contract giving the holder the right, but not the obligation, to buy or sell some item at a stated price before a stated time.

Out-of-the-money An out-of-the-money option is the opposite of an *in-the-money* option. For *calls* an option is out-of-the-money when the *strike price* exceeds the underlying item price. For *puts*, it's the reverse, implying no incentive to exercise.

Participation agreements Participation agreements (PAs) are similar in some respects to *collars*. PAs involve both *caps* and *floors* and are zero cost securities. The difference lies in the strike amount being the same, but the quantity of caps does not equal the quantity of floors.

Payoff diagram A payoff diagram is a graphical means to illustrate either (1) the value of a security (*option, stock, futures,* and so forth), (2) the dollar profit or loss, or both (1) and (2), and it relates to the value of the underlying asset at maturity.

Periodic gap The *gap* analysis report used to measure the interest rate sensitivity of *rate sensitive assets* and *rate sensitive liabilities*. The periods are also referred to as maturity buckets. The sum of individual gaps up to one year is called the cumulative gap. See *gap*.

Perpetual bond See *bond*.

Plain vanilla swap A plain vanilla *swap* is a fixed or floating *interest rate swap* with no special features.

Position Owning *option* contracts, either *long* or *short*, and either *put* or *call*.

Preferred stock A form of ownership that gives a preference over the common stockholders for dividends or assets, if the firm is dissolved.

Premium The amount the *option* buyer pays for the *option*, the current market price of the option at the time of purchase.

Present value Present value is the current value of dollars that will be received in the future.

Price risk See *investment risk*.

Principal only (POs) See *stripping*

Put option An *option* giving the holder the right to sell an item (such as a common stock) at a stated price before a stated time.

Puttable swap One *counterparty* has the right to shorten the life of the swap. This feature also gives the swap holder additional options, specifically, the option to get out of the swap at a specified amount.

Quality rating The measure of a borrower's creditworthiness. Aaa is the highest quality rating assigned to investment grade *bonds*. Bonds with the Aaa rating have the smallest degree of default risk; both the principal and interest are well protected.

Quantity risk Quantity risk refers to the uncertainty surrounding a *hedge*. That is, how likely is it that the underlying *risk* being hedged will change significantly?

Rate sensitive assets/liabilities Rate sensitivity refers to the time when the interest rate of an instrument is adjusted or *repriced*. Assets and liabilities with one year or less to maturity are considered rate sensitive. Some assets with maturities of five years or longer may also be rate sensitive.

Real interest rate The cost of borrowing without taking inflation into account. The *nominal interest rate* is the real rate of interest plus the inflation premium. The *inflation premium* represents the expected change in price levels as measured by an index, such as the Consumer Price Index.

Receive fixed counterparty One *counterparty* to the FRA will receive a fixed interest payment and pay a floating interest payment. This counterparty is referred to as the receive fixed counterparty.

Reinvestment rate The interest rate earned on cash flows received from an investment. For example, the interest payments received from a bond are (re)invested at 8 percent.

Repricing See *interest rate repricing.*

Required rate of return See *yield to maturity.*

Reset date The date on which the *floating* interest rate is set on an *FRA* or swap.

Reset frequency The number of times per year the floating rate is set, typically quarterly or semi-annually.

Residuals See *stripping bonds.*

Risk-free See *default risk.*

Settlement in arrears *Interest rate swaps* in which the cash exchanges occur one period after the floating rate is set.

Settlement price An average of futures prices near the end of the day (not the closing price). Settlement prices are used for *marking-to-market.*

Short See *Writer.*

Short hedge Short *hedges* are used to lock in the price of assets or liabilities when interest rates are expected to decline.

Short sale Short sale of futures contracts (cash commodity, security) without taking the offsetting action of buying contracts. The difference between the selling price and the buying price when the short sale is closed is the profit or loss.

Signing date The fixed interest payment on *FRAs* is set on the signing date when the contract is initiated. Typically, there are no cash flows on the signing date.

Simulation Computer-generated scenarios. They may be used to help banks evaluate interest rate risk in a dynamic environment, and for other purposes.

Spot market See *cash market.*

Spread The difference between interest rates, frequently expressed in *basis points.*

Step-up swap The *notional principal* on the swap is increased over the life of the swap. This unusual variation is applicable to banks with an increasing *gap* problem for longer maturities.

Strike price The stated price in the *option* contract. The buying price for *calls* and the selling price for *puts*.

Stripping a bond or debt security Stripping refers to separating the cash flow into interest and principal payments and selling each component individually, or in combinations. Investment bankers strip the bonds into cash flow tranches, which refer to the various interest and principal payments. In other words, interest only (IOs), and principal only (POs) payments are zero coupon type securities. Residuals are claims on any excess cash flows after payments to investors and administrative costs have been met.

Swap Rate The fixed rate of interest in the swap, also known as the *coupon* or *strike rate*.

Swaptions An *option* to enter a swap. This is one of the more popular extensions to swaps. A swaption is really an option-based product that gives you the right to enter a swap at specified terms.

Symmetric hedge is a gap hedged so that *rate sensitive assets* is equal to *rate sensitive liabilities* in order to minimize interest rate risk. This type of hedge provides a constant spread between returns on assets and interest costs, leaving *NII* unchanged. See *asymmetric hedge*.

Synthetic Derivative securities can be used to replicate the behavior of other financial instruments, loans, liabilities, etc.

Time value The time value of an option is whatever value an *option* has above its *intrinsic value*.

Tranche See *stripping*.

Writer The person selling to the option buyer; the option seller.

Yield beta The correlation coefficient obtained by regressing yield changes in a hedged instrument against yield changes in the *cheapest-to-deliver* security.

Yield curve The relationship between yields on debt securities and the years when they mature.

Yield to maturity is the average return (including interest income and capital gains or losses) over the life of the *bond*. The yield to maturity can also be thought of as the rate of return that investors require.

Zero coupon bond See *bond*.

Endnotes

1. *Commodity Trading Manual*, Chicago, IL: Chicago Board of Trade, 1985, 351.

2. *Standards of Sound Business and Financial Practices: Interest Rate Risk Management*, Canada Deposit Insurance Corporation, No Date, but about 1990.

INDEX

U

Unhedged bank's earnings
(UBE), 136
Upward side cap, 199
U.S. Department of the Treasury,
223
U.S. Treasury bill(s), 4, 31, 34, 81,
103, 119, 142, 149
see Synthetic
futures, 112, 119, 120
prices, 49-52
rates, 15
yields, 5, 49-52, 120
U.S. Treasury bonds, 91, 122-124,
149
see Cheapest
futures, 103, 110, 124
futures contracts, 105, 114
U.S. Treasury notes, 91, 116, 122,
123, 125, 149
futures, 124
U.S. Treasury securities, 30, 31
yield, 31
U.S. Treasury yield curve, 27

V

Value(s)
see Basis, Face, Fair, Franchise,
Interest rate, Interest rate
risk, Intrinsic, Market, Present, Time
additivity, 83, 93
Variable-rate loans, 9
Vietnam war, 4
Volatility, 34, 63, 108, 205
see Interest rate

W

Warning signs for directors, 223-
225
Weighted average maturity
(WAM), 241
Weighted hedge, 110-113
Weighted spreading strategies,
123
Withdrawal, 67
World War II, 3

Y

Yield, 64, 108, 125, 131
see Bond, Money, U.S.
beta, 112, 115-117
Yield curves, 27, 57, 69, 108, 117,
136, 222, 241
see U.S.
interpretation, 39-42
nonparallel changes, 123-126
risk, 241
shape, 141-142
Yield-to-maturity (YTM), 29, 32,
34, 64

Z

Zero-cost asymmetric hedges,
197-216
basics, 199-203
Zero coupon, 223
bonds, 35, 37, 60
securities, 35-38
Zero sum game, 163

About the Publisher

PROBUS PUBLISHING COMPANY

Probus Publishing Company fills the informational needs of today's business professional by publishing authoritative, quality books on timely and relevant topics, including:

- Investing
- Futures/Options Trading
- Banking
- Finance
- Marketing and Sales
- Manufacturing and Project Management
- Personal Finance, Real Estate, Insurance and Estate Planning
- Entrepreneurship
- Management

Probus books are available at quantity discounts when purchased for business, educational or sales promotional use. For more information, please call the Director, Corporate/Institutional Sales at 1-800-PROBUS-1, or write:

Director, Corporate/Institutional Sales
Probus Publishing Company
1925 N. Clybourn Avenue
Chicago, Illinois 60614
FAX (312) 868-6250